BELOW THE SURFACE

A CONFIDENCE-BUILDING FRAMEWORK TO
REACH YOUR GOALS WITHOUT OVERWHELM

KELSEA KOENREICH

A Gift For You

In this book, I refer back to time management on many occasions. It is the most common reason women don't take care of themselves or reach their goals. In order to be organized with your time, you need a plan, and I'm giving you that plan for FREE.

This is the step-by-step guide on how I run my business, my household, and my life.

Grab your guide for FREE at:

Bit.ly/TimeToolKit

Dedication

This book is dedicated to my parents for teaching me resilience, my husband for being my biggest supporter, and my children for being my greatest teachers.

"Hope is being able to see that there is light despite all of the darkness."

Desmond Tutu

Table of Contents

CHAPTER ONE

HITTING ROCK BOTTOM

My Story

Waking up in an anti-suicide smock, my stomach was sour and my head was fuzzy. I was lying in a plastic bed on the floor of what I would later learn was the medical unit. I had told the officers I was going to kill myself during the booking process. I rose to my feet, and as I stood, the gravity of my situation hit me.

I needed water. I walked to the sink and looked around to see three other women in the cell with me. It's hard to say if it was my contacts or the weathered jailhouse mirror, but everything was hazy as I stared back at myself.

What was I doing here? Why did this happen again? What am I going to do?

In that moment, I had no answers.

I stood at the door waiting for someone to come so I could ask for some contact solution. I just wanted to see and get rid of the stickiness in my eyelids from all the crying I had done the night before.

At some point, a conversation started between us inmates. I was asked the charges I was brought in for. A DUI and a felony drug charge, my first felony. The weight of everything was too heavy, so I distracted myself by continuing the conversation with the other women. Two of them had been arrested for murder, and the other was going through withdrawals from her continued drug use right before our eyes.

I listened to their stories and tried to play it cool, as if I wasn't scared shitless of being in this place or terrified of what would happen next. Next, there was a woman accused of shooting and killing her ex-husband, then a mother accused of drowning her own children.

Finally, I got contact solution, glad for the slight clarity it would bring to my life. Back to the sink I went, back to the mirror where I was forced to look at myself again. I don't think there was any amount of solution that could strip the lenses of whatever they had on them, but I rinsed and put them back in anyway.

Then I stood, staring back into my own eyes, my head spinning with questions. At twenty-three years old, this was my third time in jail. This was the third time I had gotten caught in the span of four years, which was such a small number in comparison to all the illegal activities I was involved in.

Was someone bailing me out? How will I tell my parents? What the hell am I going to do?

Suddenly, everything became clear. If I continued on my current path, it would end sooner than I wanted. If I didn't change, I would end up here again—or, truthfully, I would probably die. I had to make a choice.

I decided in that moment I didn't want to die. I didn't want to come back to this place. I wanted to go home. I wanted to live. I had no idea what my next step was. I just knew this wasn't the end.

Tiny fragments of the night before came back to me. Driving after a long day of drinking to get something to eat. The lights in my rearview mirror flashing. My heart racing. Still being in my swimsuit from visiting the beach that day, dropping my bottoms on the sidewalk to pee in front of the officer instead of attempting to walk the straight line. Slipping out of my handcuffs in the back seat of the cop car as if I was going to just walk free. Being soaked in my own urine.

Hysterical tears as I was being walked through the booking process. Sitting down with medical personnel and answering the question, "Do you want to harm yourself?" with an absolute yes. Just like many times before, life felt too hard to handle. I wanted my life to end. In those moments, it was the end of the road for me, and rightfully so, because there was absolutely no way I had enough strength to move forward.

I was bailed out, luckily. When I was released, an overflow of emotions hit me, as if I had been stripped raw and had to start life all over again. There was no comfort in that county jail, but there was no comfort out in the open either.

That was my third and final arrest in May of 2010. It was the worst and best day of my life. It was the rock bottom that I needed to live through to see that I was meant for more. It was the lowest point of my life but also the point that caused me to make a change. Ten years later, I have no doubt that if that arrest hadn't happened I wouldn't be here.

Your Journey Below The Surface

I shared this story to help you understand the depth of my darkness, and to tell you that you can rise from your own darkness—whatever it looks like. Your story might be similar to mine, or it might not be, but I know you've felt hopeless before, and I'm here to tell you that there is always hope. What once was a life filled with shame, pain, and disgust is now a life of joy, trust, and accomplishment for me. I believe you are capable of having that too.

The road to finding my purpose and uncovering who I was meant to be wasn't easy. The work that I've done has been gritty. I am resilient, just like you. If you've made it through anything hard in your life, you have the ability to do this work too. I know that you can think of a tragic moment in your life. When you look back, you can't believe you endured the pain, but here you are, on the other side of it.

I don't believe that we ever stop facing obstacles. Instead, we learn how to navigate them by gathering skills and tools that change our perspectives. I believe in my abilities enough now to say that I am unbreakable because of the foundation I've built, and I want to teach you how to rise from your rock bottom and build that foundation for yourself. You start by facing your darkness. In the first years of my transformation, I chose to use my darkness as a reminder of the place I never wanted to return—even on the days when I was tempted. The darkness will always remain; you will become strong enough to choose the light instead.

It is my purpose and my mission to be a glimmer of hope for you. That is what kept me moving forward as I started my journey. I had hope that there was something more to life without knowing what that was. I have felt anxiety, stress, overwhelm, and heartbreak, but I continue to choose gratitude for this path that has led me here, to you.

You are worthy of a life that is fulfilling, meaningful, powerful, and full of joy. What you need is to build a foundation that you can fall back on when the days are overwhelming, stressful, and when you feel as if another minute in your situation seems impossible. What you will build is a belief in yourself so solid that even on your worst days you know there is still hope.

I am going to walk you through changes I made in my own life to build the foundation I stand strongly upon now, and I am going to tell you why you need to make these changes. I will also tell you what happens if you don't make these changes, because I'm not here to sugarcoat things for you. At the end of each chapter, you will find action steps to follow. Reading and connecting with the message on these pages will be a powerful experience, but taking this information and applying it will be life-changing.

As you continue throughout this book, close your eyes. When my words meet your heart, know that I am walking through this with you. I know that our situations may not be the same, but I've walked through the fire before, and I'll walk through it again with you.

There are six steps to building a foundation:

1. *Pick a site.*
   This is where you choose yourself and are able to see the value you bring to this universe.

2. *Survey the lot.*

   This requires you to be honest about where you are and own your story.

3. *Start digging.*

   Once you've owned who you are fully, you can start digging to uncover your dreams and establish where you want to be.

4. *Install footings.*

   After your goals are established, I will walk you through the five anchors of stability, your footings.

5. *Seal footings.*

   To seal these footings in place, I will walk you through how to create and break habits.

6. *Build walls.*

   After your habits are created, you will reflect and build walls with momentum.

Even when that next step feels scary, you'll build confidence by facing your fears along the way.

Let's build.

CHAPTER TWO

PICK A SITE

Seeing Your Value

When I was younger, usually in a drunken conversation, I would tell people that I had no desire to get married or have children. I know there are women out there that have their weddings planned before they meet their partners. They know how many kids they will have and what all of their names will be. I was not one of those women, not because I didn't actually want those things but because I told myself I didn't deserve them.

In my eyes, people who got married and had children were "normal." I had labeled myself as anything but normal,.I convinced myself that I actually enjoyed my partying lifestyle. Marriage and children weren't goals of mine, and my behavior reflected that. I didn't let people get too close, and if they did, I made sure I pushed them away somehow. It's easy for me to look back on this now and connect the dots. Many therapy sessions later, it was nothing more than a story I was telling myself about my value.

Deep in my heart, I wanted to be connected with someone, but I had to believe I was worth being connected with first. As I write this now, I am happily married to Eric. Since celebrating our union in 2012, I still have days where I am in disbelief that he chose me. Oh, and about not having children, I have two of them, so I guess you could say that story I was telling myself was pretty far off.

It wasn't that I didn't want a loving relationship prior to meeting Eric, but without the belief that I deserved love, the men I pursued had no desire to love me either. I didn't want anyone to be too close, but I definitely didn't want to be alone. In fact, being abandoned was one of my biggest fears.

My choices in men were a reflection of how I felt about myself, which meant I was constantly picking men that didn't treat me well or had no interest in being committed to me. I was forever chasing multiple men, and always putting myself in situations where I was seen as unlovable. I wanted love, attention, and care, but I gave none of these things to myself. At that time, I didn't really understand why I made these choices. All I understood was that I didn't want to be alone. I didn't really care who kept me company or what I would have to put myself through in order to get their attention.

Having someone that I actually called a boyfriend was rare, but there was one—whose name was also Eric—that I believe was my first experience of love. It was the first relationship in my young age that I felt accepted. I didn't feel like I needed to hide who I was. Our relationship was rocky, but I cared deeply for him.

We had been dating for a few months, and one morning in September of 2004, I got a call from a friend. I still remember her exact words, "Have you heard about Eric?" I don't remember exactly what my reply was, but I told her that I hadn't heard from him. Her response was short and lacked emotion, "He's dead." And what I remember from there was dropping to my knees on the tile floor and screaming. It was as if my world had ended in that moment. He was nineteen years old when he died, and I was sixteen—both of us with so much life left to live, and yet I was the only one still here. He was found floating in a pool at a friend's house, an ending that still fills my head with questions to this day.

His death was like fuel to a fire. It was an excuse to numb myself with drugs and alcohol. I became the victim, vowing to never love anyone again. His death was my excuse to drive ninety miles per hour on a path of destruction.

From that point, there were a lot of men. My life became simply about serving whatever need I had at that time. Many times, the only thing I wanted was to not be alone. I continued to find myself in situations where I wasn't being respected. I had no boundaries. I would be heartbroken and wonder time and time again, *Why am I alone?* I would wake up not remembering the night before, and not knowing the person in my bed. I was fueled by hate for myself. The shame piled on and continued the cycle. I feared ever sharing this part of me with anyone.

The most powerful thing that I've ever done for myself after hitting my rock bottom was seeking help through therapy and life coaching. It was through these experiences that I realized the missing piece was my ability to see the value in myself. I learned that the reason why I continued to seek a companion who was not aligned with my values was because I didn't know who I was, where I was going, or what my values even were.

The most important realization was that I was expecting these men to respect me and treat me respectfully when I didn't do that for myself. I looked at myself as this broken human with missing pieces. I was dinged up and shattered, and because of that view, I believed I wasn't valuable enough to love. I treated myself as if I was broken and unfixable, and therefore, I was getting exactly what I deserved. Everything rested on seeing my value and understanding that I went through these experiences, but they didn't define me.

I finally learned through this personal work that I was still valuable. I was able to see that I deserved respect from others and that I could learn to respect myself. I recognized I could treat myself in a way that aligned with my values, once I knew what my values were. This was possible once I recognized that my experiences didn't define me. I was able to turn my past into power, going from being embarrassed to empowered. This was picking my site. This was choosing myself.

It is one thing to say you deserve something, but knowing in your heart that you deserve something and acting as if you truly believe that changes your world. You start to shift into prioritizing yourself and stop living for everyone else. This shift is a difficult one for many. I am sure you see yourself as valuable because of what you can do for others—but how are you treating yourself?

The choices that you make in every area of your life are reflective of how you feel about yourself. Let that sink in.

I know that you've set boundaries in your head before, but have been too scared to speak up about them. I know you've been in the shame spiral of breaking promises to yourself over and over again. I know that you've made a choice, repeatedly, that you don't feel proud of, but you continue to make that choice because you've taught yourself to believe it's who you are.

I know that you've consciously made decisions that disappoint you because you want to put everyone else before yourself.

Seeing your value is not about thinking that you're the greatest thing to walk this earth. It is about understanding who you are and honoring your values. Prioritizing yourself is knowing what's important to you and respecting that. You are able to own who you are fully and wholeheartedly in order to make choices that reflect your values. You've told yourself many times that you're going to choose differently, you're not going to let a man talk to you that way anymore, you're not going to offer help when you already feel overwhelmed, or you're not going to put yourself in the same situation that made you frustrated last week. Your intentions are to change, to do better. Your intentions are to be better.

This requires self-respect, as well seeing your own value. To truly recognize all you have to offer, you have to understand that the choices that seem so surface level aren't going to come easy to you at first. To make those choices easier, you have to do one thing: you have to choose you. You have to choose yourself over and over again, even when you are scared of who you will disappoint.

This is the hardest step for people to take, especially women. You live to serve other people, you serve in your relationships, you serve in the workplace, you just serve and give and serve and give. Putting yourself first doesn't seem like an option because your calendar is so full, there's no place to add anything. You're so exhausted and overwhelmed with everything in your day-to-day life that putting yourself first is impossible.

I need to tell you something honestly, though. Your inability to choose yourself is keeping you from who you are meant to be. Prioritizing yourself allows you to see you're worth all the hard choices, boundaries, and rejections.

Choosing Yourself

When you start making those small choices, your confidence will grow and your worth will become clear.

There is a misconception that choosing to put yourself first means that you are disregarding other people's feelings, or disregarding other people altogether. Choosing yourself doesn't mean disregarding other people. Choosing yourself means making choices based on what is important to you, what your values are, and what fulfills you. When you are fulfilled, and your cup is full, it will run over into how you treat others. This means that sometimes you will still choose to serve other people. For example, as a mother, you take care of your children even when it's hard. The difference is by choosing yourself and knowing how valuable you are, you know when to take breaks, you know when to set boundaries, and you know when to ask for help.

The misconception that you're selfish if you choose yourself has been passed down through generations. Many of our parents told us, "Don't be selfish," or "You are being so selfish right now." We have this ingrained thought that doing anything for ourselves is selfish.

And it allows us to make excuses. We don't want to be selfish, so we aren't even kind to ourselves in the smallest ways.

I'm choosing to see the word selfish differently, and you can, too. If somebody wants to call me selfish, I let them because I respect myself. The conscious choices that you make allow you to see the value that you hold. This gives you space to be a better mother, leader, wife, sister, and friend. When I am given the options of either being "selfish" and taking care of myself or doing something that is not respecting my values, I think of it like this. Being selfish leads to my happiness, my fulfillment, and living my true purpose. Beyond that, it leads to more self-love, which means that I can be more loving in all of my relationships. Choosing to put others first and not respect myself leads to feelings of resentment, impatience, anger, and the tendency to blame my position on other people.

The first thing that will stop you from choosing yourself is always going to be fear. As a personal development coach working specifically with women to overcome obstacles and prioritize themselves, I see this fear show up in every client. We have this deeply ingrained misconception that if we take care of ourselves, we are abandoning everyone else. The shift to seeing ourselves as valuable enough to choose first takes time and guidance, which is why I walk through this with the women I work with. When I'm talking to my clients about this shift, the fear of disappointing other people is always an obstacle we have to overcome. No matter which option you choose, you might disappoint someone. You're just so used to being fearful of disappointing someone else that you don't even realize the person you disappoint is always yourself. Ask yourself, do I want to be the person that disappoints myself? If you don't care about disappointing yourself, you aren't understanding the value that you have.

I know you're scared about what others will think. "If I choose this school, my parents are going to be mad." "If I make this parenting choice, my sister is going to be mad." Do you want to spend the rest of your life making decisions based on whether you might possibly make someone upset? That was the life I lived, bowing down to anyone and everyone that was in front of me.

You are capable of living differently. You are capable of serving yourself in a way that allows you to also give to others. You just have it backward right now, which is why you end up in a place of constant overwhelm. Your fear of disappointing others holds you back from making decisions that align with where you want to be.

The enlightenment that comes when you see that you are disappointing someone regardless of the path you choose—and that that person should not always be yourself—is enough for you to start choosing differently. I'm promising you right now that you're always going to disappoint people. There's always going to be somebody that doesn't like you. There will be someone who doesn't like the choices that you make. Take peace in knowing you can let that go by consistently making choices that show the respect you have for yourself.

Finding Clarity In Your Choices

You've opened your eyes and realized that you need to come first, and now I am giving you tools you can use to live a better life.

Something else that stops us from choosing ourselves is the lack of clarity. Consistently choosing other people over yourself and not seeing the value that you have prevents you from seeing what's important to you. I've talked to countless mothers who dive in fully to motherhood and completely lose themselves. They have no hobbies and aren't even sure of what they like anymore. That is a loss of clarity.

You lose sight of the dreams you had when you were younger. You have no time in your day-to-day life to even think about them. You're so wrapped up in serving other people, you've forgotten yourself. You don't really consider the long-term effects of the actions you take. It's all about making the best decision that you can at that moment. I truly believe that most times we are doing the best we can with the tools we have.

I want you to think about when you were young, and there was nothing blocking you from your dreams. Go back to a time when you could dream bigger because your imagination was endless. You are worth the time and effort of making those dreams a reality. You are valuable beyond measure. You deserve to live a life you feel proud of, full of things that fulfill you.

Life is crazy. You are busy. I get it. You've got work, kids, and all the social things that you're committing yourself to. Let me be honest with you, all the things that you're putting in your calendar that aren't for you are just distracting you. Putting yourself on the back burner is going to block you from all the dreams that you have and leave you unfulfilled.

You get *one* life. Please understand that you are valuable and worthy enough to put yourself first. You are deserving of great things, and it's time to move forward.

How to see your value:

1. *Take ownership and responsibility for where you are right now.*
When I knew it was time for me to change the way I was living my life, I went through the victim phase. I blamed the person who initiated my third arrest, because if they hadn't called on me, I would have never gone to jail. It was easy for me to say it was all his fault. I was unwilling to see it as a gift at that moment.

It wasn't until I shifted my perspective that I had the realization that it was my actions that earned me that suicide smock, and I drank every sip of the alcohol that day. I chose to put myself behind the wheel of that car that day, and if he hadn't called and gotten me arrested, I may not have made it home without crashing. The choices that put me in jail were all mine.

There is power in taking ownership of your choices. There is not a single person that you can place the blame on for your position. You carry experiences with you from your life, but they don't define you. I know that you have been through hard things. I want you to recognize that everything you go through, you choose what you want to do with it. When you step up and you say, "I'm here because I got myself here," it is powerful. It means that you're aware of where you are, and that you realize you can choose to do things differently.

Stop playing the blame game and understand you have the power to choose another path.

2. *Turn your failures into lessons.*

I can't tell you how many failures I've had. They are impossible to count. I've had relationship failures, business failures, and broken many promises to myself. I can look at each time I've failed and pick out something I learned. Taking my last arrest as an example, I learned that I was living my life in a way that would not get me where I wanted to go. That knowledge is powerful, a tool I can use to guide my choices.

Look back on all the challenges that you've had in your life. Put yourself back in those hard places. Open your eyes and realize what you have learned from it. See that as a blessing. If you change your perspective about the things that you've been through, it takes you from being a victim to being empowered. You don't have to be the sad little girl that went through that thing. You can be the strong little girl that overcame that thing.

3. *Go to where your power is.*

I feel so good after I work out. Even during my workouts I feel strong and powerful. I've always loved building strength and challenging myself. Pushing myself to an extreme place, where I feel like I can't do it anymore, and then I do it anyway. That's a place of power for me, and that's why I repeat that workout so often.

Where is the place that fills you with confidence, the place that when you're there or when you're done you feel unstoppable? That's where you have to go. Spend more time there. Putting yourself back in those hard places will allow you to see how you came out on the other side.

If you don't know what that place is because you haven't felt what power feels like in so long, try speaking up, setting a boundary, or trying something new just to say you can or you did. You can expand the power and the value that you see in yourself by putting yourself in positions where you can feel it more frequently.

4. *Keep promises to yourself.*

Every time I woke up hungover, not remembering the day before, I promised myself I was going to do things differently. I would tell myself I wasn't going to drink that day. I wasn't going to go to that bar anymore. I wasn't going to hang out with that friend anymore. Promise after promise that I didn't fulfill. I had the habit of never doing what I said I would do.

Keeping promises to yourself seems like something small, but it's one of the most valuable things you can do. You can start small by saying you're going to wear a certain bracelet every day, or get up five minutes earlier so you can write down three things you are grateful for every day. The point isn't just to do whatever the promise is; it's simply to build momentum and show yourself that you can do something that you say you're going to do.

Once you start keeping promises to yourself, you build a habit of following through with action. This develops into becoming a person who values themselves. You become someone who sets a goal, plans it out, and does it. Your self-worth and confidence develops when you consistently take action to follow your words. It creates power.

5. *Lead by example.*

When I started my first online business as a fitness coach, I transitioned into a leadership role without recognizing that I was being a leader. My intent was to help people. I just wanted people to feel better. Being a coach for so many years, I realize how powerful it is to treat myself like I would treat a friend and to continue to lead by example. Now, as a personal development coach, I teach women how to live with confidence and jump off the hamster wheel of overwhelm to take action in their lives. On days where I may not feel like doing something that is valuable to me, I do it anyway. I know that doing things that are fulfilling to me will make me a better leader, and teach others to do the same.

My belief is that we are all leaders in some way. If you are a mother, your children are watching. In your workplace, people admire your work. Regardless of what your job title is, someone is watching. You can help and teach others, but what kind of example are you teaching if you don't do the things you tell others to do? If you want to see your value, treat yourself well and teach others to do the same. Watching people become empowered using the tools that you've given them is one of the greatest experiences you will ever go through.

Chapter Summary:

- The choices you make are reflective of how you feel about yourself.
- Let go of telling yourself you are selfish for choosing yourself.
- Continuing to put your needs, wants, and dreams on the back burner will block you from pursuing what you are meant for and leave you feeling resentful.

- When you fear disappointing someone else, remember that not prioritizing yourself is disappointing you.
- Prioritizing others' needs over your own will lead you to constant overwhelm, stress, and lack of clarity.
- Choosing you allows you to get clarity on your value and doesn't mean that you disregard others.

CHAPTER THREE

SURVEY THE LOT

Owning Your Story

I suffered from anxiety and feared what people would think about me for more than fifteen years of my life. To be honest, I still feel the fear sometimes. It was such a long streak of time where I made so many embarrassing mistakes that it made me feel that I was worthless. It was impossible to see any sort of value in myself, just like we discussed in chapter two.

I got glasses in third grade, and started to gain weight around that time. I followed it up with getting braces in middle school, and I disliked everything about my appearance. I tried to cover that hate by numbing the pain with food. I found the numbing effects of drugs and alcohol in high school. Until the past few years, I can't remember a time in my life when I didn't feel ashamed of my looks, weight, or drug abuse.

I searched for acknowledgement from men from a young age, writing love letters to boys in middle school that would laugh at me. When my virginity was taken without consent from me at the age of fourteen, I learned I could use my body for attention, and that led me to a highly sexualized path. This was also a source of shame.

Instead of peeling back what felt like never-ending layers of embarrassment and shame, I ignored them. I used numerous coping mechanisms: food, sex, drugs, and alcohol. The more I used them, the more I was able to justify my choices. In each instance, I could normalize it by surrounding myself with similar people, or not showing the people around me who I truly was. It was easier to pack the pain in boxes and store them away than to think about opening them. Any time I would have a conversation with somebody new, I felt there was no reason to bring up my past at all. I wouldn't speak about my history, my relationships, or being arrested multiple times. Every conversation I had with a stranger filled me with fear and anxiety. I lived in so much shame that it became something that stopped me from moving forward. I was stuck.

I didn't see my experiences as lessons until I was on the other side of my rock bottom. I didn't truly recognize the shame I had or the volume of trauma I had been through until I cracked everything open, one layer at a time. With consistent effort and a large amount of time, I started the transition from embarrassed to empowered.

Something really fascinating happened during this transition. I started to see the lessons in my failures and realized that what I walked through was a necessary part of my growth. It seemed like a huge leap to hide in shame one day and be so open with my story on another, but like any other transition, it was not something that happened overnight.

When I talk about building your foundation and surveying the lot, I'm talking about taking every piece of your life and acknowledging it. With that acknowledgment, comes acceptance, and with acceptance, we can make a change. This is how we start to transition to the proud part of our stories. We see that we have an advantage because of our experiences.

Prior to attending therapy and learning why I was making the choices I was making, I lived in isolation because I was so embarrassed about my mistakes. Facing who I was and the choices I had made seemed too hard. It was too heavy of a burden. What I hadn't realized was that not only was I still carrying that burden despite trying to lock it away, but now it had me stuck and unable to move forward in many areas of my life.

I came to a point of having a choice once again: Do I want to live my life in this state of embarrassment and isolation because I'm so scared of admitting who I am? The other option was to accept that my experiences were things that I went through and did not define who I was. This is what owning your story means. And with the help of a therapist, I opened every box I had stored away.

I am sure you are wondering what accepting yourself will look like and if it's even possible to accept yourself. This is an overwhelming feeling when you feel as if you've packed away too many boxes to count, and I want you to know that you don't have to unpack them alone. Without the guidance of therapy and life coaching, I wouldn't have been able to make the transition from being ashamed to fully accepting my story.

It's very hard in the moment to think about something like abusing your body or repeatedly ending up in jail as something you can be proud of, but this is what owning your story means. I don't have to be proud of the acts themselves, but I can be proud that I am strong enough to have made it to the other side. Each thing that embarrasses you, you are on the other side of.

You have to start small. Accept each part of your story individually and build on those steps. I stand in a place where I can openly talk about everything that I've been through, many years later, without shame. Don't adopt the unrealistic expectation that you can be in this place overnight. It takes time, and every step matters. I was kept from moving forward with relationships, and in seeking a career. Once you open your eyes to the weight you are carrying from that shame, you can see what you are being held back from. As Dr. Brené Brown explains, shame can't live in light. You have to bring it to the surface, and I want to give you some guidance on how to do that.

First, I want you to recognize you are unique and different in an unmatched way. There is not one single person in this universe that has the exact same story and skill set that you have. This is so powerful because it allows you to see that you hold value in a way that nobody else does. Our similarities help us build connections with people, and our differences allow us to help teach people. With this perspective, you recognize that you are a leader. This recognition is an important part of owning your story. When you hide behind a barrier of shame, it's a disservice to everyone around you.

I'm not saying that you have to open up and share your story with the world, but speaking your truth will move you forward. The vulnerability that is required may be a challenge for you, as it is difficult to be honest with yourself and to take ownership for where you are. But what comes from this action is freedom and a step toward becoming who you are meant to be. You will be fully aware of what is going on and how you're actually feeling. You will get clarity on the things you want to change or how you want to be better. The hardest part is getting honest about where you are, but the beautiful part is what comes when you open the door to what that truth brings. You will finally see where you are and realize that you have power over your actions.

Something I did in my own process of owning my story was separating the boxes, the different experiences and parts of myself. I took steps by speaking about one area, but then found other areas that I wanted to keep hidden. I noticed that there were things that kept coming up in my life that showed me areas that needed to be addressed.

There are parts of each of our stories that we are okay with. You can admit that you had a traumatic childhood, or that you explored with alcohol and drugs, or possibly that, as an adult, you repeated the behaviors you saw growing up. There are the parts that feel a little gritty, maybe your first arrest or getting too drunk and doing something you regret. You were able to overcome that experience and talk about it, but then there are things you keep hidden, parts of the story that are missing. My hidden piece was always my sexual story. I could openly talk about things like my arrest and my drug and alcohol use, but I never wanted to admit things that I did with my body.

We are really good at separating experiences and compartmentalizing different feelings. I am sure you bring up things in conversation that you are confident about, hoping that they overshadow the parts you don't feel so good about. The truth is that everybody has those dark parts. Everybody has things that they hope to keep in the boxes, tucked away. When you address them, your fear of being seen is overcome. Even when you feel the fear—as I still do—you are able to proceed anyway. Imagine finally being able to feel like there is nothing that anybody can say about you that you don't already own. Owning your story means that you fully understand each part of you. Everyone has both light and dark experiences in their own stories. This is what makes us able to better understand each other. We are unique in our own ways and able to talk about our experiences, and this is what builds connections.

Past choices can cause you to carry a significant amount of guilt. I want you to recognize again that you are not the things that happened to you, the experiences that you went through, or the struggles that you faced. They are an important piece of who you are, but they don't define you.

Your identity is not defined by your experiences. This is what caused the huge shift for me. I was able to see that I could go through these hard things. I could navigate through them even when I was scared. You can admit things that you've done and come out on top because you can see how all of those things actually served you. If you don't have acceptance or acknowledgement for the things that you've been through, you will never be able to live fully in the purpose that you were meant for.

You will carry these past experiences with you forever, but you have a choice. You get to choose whether you carry them and hide them in shame, or carry them and see them as lessons. If you choose to use them as lessons, you can use them in a way that will make you better. The choice to use them to make you better will inspire others to do the same. You have to accept and acknowledge these lessons and the failures that you've had. You can then change your perspective to see the opportunity that was created from that failure. Without my third arrest, I wouldn't be here married with two children running the business of my dreams.

I am a Brené Brown superfan. If you haven't read her books, go buy them. One of her most powerful quotes, in my opinion, is, "Shame cannot survive being spoken. It cannot survive empathy." You don't realize the impact of this until you feel it, until you actually walk through owning each of those pieces and you see what bringing them to the surface really means. When you finally speak about the thing that you're afraid of sharing, you feel a physical weight being lifted off of you. I experienced this so many times. You don't even realize sometimes the weight of these things on you, but like I said, you carry them with you despite being packed away. Most of us do the opposite of what we need to. We say horrible things to ourselves and think that these experiences are so negative, we could never possibly admit to them. When you own who you are, you start to understand yourself, and when you build an understanding of yourself, you're able to offer empathy. When you offer empathy, like Brené Brown explains, shame can't survive there.

It's similar to when you work out. You may really not want to go to the gym, but when you show up, you're never going to regret it. The empowerment that comes with owning your story and letting go of that shame is a similar endorphin rush that follows a workout. It's this overwhelming sense of that weight being lifted so that you can finally be in a certain situation without feeling like you're hiding part of yourself.

Maybe you've said before that you have a wall up, and that it's hard to break down because you've been hurt in the past. We all have those walls, but walls, much like obstacles and challenges, are meant to be broken through or climbed over. When you understand that isolating and hiding in that shame is preventing you from getting relief, you can stop blocking yourself from the love you deserve.

Here's what happens when you own your story. After the initial endorphin rush, the weight releases each time you share a certain part of your story. The lightness that you feel in your body turns to clarity. All these things that you've been hiding require darkness. Your visions that were cloudy become clear. When you look into your own eyes, the haziness starts to fade. You can't expect for doors to open and to see things clearly with all this darkness in your way. Owning your story provides the clarity that allows you to take steps toward things you were afraid of before. You start to walk into rooms with more confidence, unafraid of someone finding out who you really are. This confidence will show up in every single area of your life: your relationships have a deeper connection, your success lasts longer, and your belief in yourself is finally there. What happens in this shift is you actually start to see the world differently. You're looking forward instead of standing still, and you can see possibility in your life. These chains that have been holding you down and keeping you stuck are starting to be removed. You see that you're capable of trying new things and experimenting with life. You can explore the world around you without fear. You become limitless. You become brave.

How to own your story:

1. *Acknowledge it.*

I was sitting in my bed after getting home from my third time being arrested, and my final rock bottom. I can still picture myself crying so heavily knowing that everything was going to have to change. I couldn't believe that I had gotten myself there once again. And in that moment, I knew that I needed help and that if I was going to do things differently, I needed to learn how.

This is where therapy and life coaching came in. With the the help of these women, I was finally able to acknowledge the pieces of my story. I was finally able to recognize that there were parts of me that I was hiding. Awareness is always the first step. Once you become aware of something, you then have to acknowledge that it's real. Look at your story, go back through your experiences, and acknowledge that each of these experiences happened, but none of them define who you are.

2. *Speak it.*

After you're aware of these experiences and you recognize and acknowledge that there are parts that you are hiding, you can speak them. This is where, again, having guidance from some sort of mentor or professional comes in. You need someone to listen, and a space where you can just be heard.

I remember in the starting parts of therapy that I would hold back a little bit. I wasn't ready to be fully seen, but the more that I showed up for myself, the more layers I could peel back. You can do the same. It's okay to go one layer at a time. And if there are parts of you that you are ashamed of, speaking them will give you that release that I'm talking about.

3. *Write it.*

Everyone is a different kind of writer; some are note-takers, some make lists, and then some journal every single day as if their lives depended on it. It doesn't matter what kind of writer you are; writing is powerful. When I decided I wanted to write a book, there were so many years after that I didn't want to put pen to paper. I just didn't really know where to start. Now, looking back, I can understand that there were still parts of my story that I needed to own before I could write this for you. The truth is that this book isn't just for you. Oh, it's for me, too.

Write down your experiences, let them stare back at you from the paper. They can't hurt you. What happens when we get this visual feedback is that it does bring us a little bit of that clarity. We start to separate it from us and realize just what it is—something that we walked through and not who we are.

4. *Share it.*

Who you share with and how you share your experiences depends on your comfort level. I didn't go from being ashamed of all these parts of my story directly to writing a book or announcing it on social media. I wasn't able to just wake up one day and feel fully confident in my ability to use my story in a way that would help others. It took time. Sharing with a therapist first allowed me to see that I could speak my story without the fear of being judged.

What happens when we share in areas other than therapy offices is that when our walls come down, so do other people's. We put something out there with fear because we want to be seen, and then if even one person says, "I see you," there comes a flood of relief from knowing that we're not alone. Maybe for you this is just sharing with a friend or partner, but when you share something that weighs heavily on you with someone that you love, it will make your relationship stronger.

5. *Use it.*

If you would have told me that day I woke up in the medical unit of the county jail that I would be able to use that experience to move forward in my own life, I would have called you a liar. But here I am. On the other side. If I hadn't gone through all of my experiences and traumas, I wouldn't have my business. I wouldn't be writing this book. I probably wouldn't have most of the things or people that are in my life.

Look into each of your experiences and write them down so you can see them. Then ask yourself: What lesson did I take away? There is someone out there that's sitting in that same place looking for that lesson.

Chapter Summary:

- You are unique. There is no one with the same story and skills as you.
- There are parts of us that we feel proud of and parts we don't; each are equally important.
- Your experiences are just that; they aren't who you are.

- Shame can't live in light. Bringing it out of the darkness gives us clarity.
- Sharing your truth allows you to connect with others and feel empowered.
- Owning your story will give you a different perspective of the world.

CHAPTER FOUR

START DIGGING

Achieving Your Goals

I want to fast-forward in my personal story here a bit. We've talked about my rock bottom and different ways I was not taking care of myself, and I've shared about owning all the pieces of my story. When I talk about the clarity that comes from accepting who you are and where you are, I know this only because I've walked through it. It's hard to say whether the opportunities were always there and I was unable to see them, or if I just finally valued myself enough to work toward becoming what I was meant to be.

In this chapter, I want to talk about the business side of my life, the process of building my career and the success I've been able to achieve because of owning, and sharing, my story.

I am a coach and speaker working with women all over the world. I teach women how to embrace themselves and live confidently. The rise to this leadership position has been a long process of trying and failing.

When I started on the path of entrepreneurship, I didn't even know what I was doing or where I was headed, but I trusted in myself and my ability to persist. When I thought about my goals, I felt like I was at the base of a mountain, with no idea what the mountaintop looked like, or what tools I would need to climb it.

To be honest with you, I didn't have a lot of clarity over where exactly I wanted to be, and I think a lot of people feel this. I was only clear on one thing: I wanted to help people. This was why I was drawn to fitness as a start to my career. I was filled with a passion and desire to make others feel better physically.

As children, we have dreams about wanting to become a doctor, a veterinarian, or firefighter. We wear costumes and play pretend with stuffed animals, serving them tea or doctoring them up. For me, the only memory I have of wanting to grow into something was repeatedly saying I wanted to be president. Not of the book club or my school council, President of the United States. I wasn't worried about how I was going to get there; it was all about holding on to something that felt important to me, something I felt called to do.

It makes sense to me now, looking back on it. From a young age, I wanted to be a leader without knowing what leadership even was. As I grew older, the dream was pushed to the side until it was eventually forgotten, just like many of our goals are. I was so clouded by my own judgement and numbed from not being able to follow through with any goal. I was blind to the skills I had. I eventually stopped exploring my interests.

You likely have the expectation that when you set a goal you should be consistently motivated, that you should be excited and driven to move forward at all times. I call that bullshit. The expectation that we need to feel motivated in order to act on our goals is what leads us to being paralyzed. I want to share what I've learned through my own experiences and taught thousands of women.

I want you to get very clear about your goal. Having a specific goal is extremely important, but don't let the specificity of a goal be your excuse not to move forward. Even when you feel like you know the exact desired end result, there will likely be some variance in your experience. If you don't know the specific end result that you want, or what goal to set, start with where you are and set a goal on who you want to be, or how you want to feel. If you want to lose weight but don't know a realistic amount, set a goal to eat in a way that makes you feel proud, and then get specific on what that means.

I can confidently say that I don't know exactly what the next five or ten years will look like. Do any of us, really? The truth is I know where I started. I know how far I've come. And I know that I will continue to rise. When you build belief in yourself and never give up, you will continue to reach your goals. Goal setting is much more than checking boxes off a list; it is consistently showing up for yourself along the journey.

When I started in the fitness industry in 2011, I was making seven dollars a session. If you were looking for proof that money isn't everything when it comes to fulfillment in your career, there you go. The pay sucked, the hours sucked, but the people were real and the opportunity to rise was there.

Since committing to developing my true self, I believe I've developed a growth mindset, sometimes even to a fault. Having a growth mindset is believing your talents can be developed through hard work, good planning, and feedback along the way. I always feel the pull of wanting to do more. Within those seven-dollar sessions, I vowed to create a life-changing experience for clients while also planning my next move. I wanted to be present where I was, thankful for where I'd come from, and I wanted to look forward to what I could still do. I rebuilt trust with myself and kept my promises. This allowed me to build a belief in myself that meant if I said I was going to do something, I did it.

I didn't go from making seven dollars a session to running my own successful business overnight. There was a massive amount of little steps, mentors, and most importantly, failures along the way. It's so easy to expect instant gratification. You think that because you started you should be instantly rewarded. You continue to quit because you aren't checking off those boxes, even though you might be achieving goals you didn't know you even had. You have to start somewhere, but you also have to keep going.

I didn't see my life goal clearly when I worked in fitness making seven dollars a session, but I felt that glimmer of hope, and I honored that. Your goals don't have to be—and shouldn't be—based on what someone else wants for you. We have natural instincts and abilities we have to honor. I am so thankful that I've continued to honor and follow all of these different paths. Each path was filled with lessons that were necessary to move forward. I want you to know that whatever your view of success is, you are able to achieve it.

The Mindset Behind Reaching Your Goals

I don't think there's enough stress on the importance of clarity within our goals. You can read about methods on how to set goals in action steps. You start with a big goal, you put together a plan, you break it down into small steps, you follow the steps, and there you are. It seems simple enough, right? But what happens if you don't know what the end goal is? Ask yourself, "Where do I want to be?" Do you have an answer? The answers come when you start digging.

For many people, the answer would simply be, anywhere but where I am right now. Goal setting and achieving has to be more than the surface-level plan on paper. You want to be better, you want to be stronger, you want to be more successful, you want to be happier, but how can you set a goal around something that you can't visualize? The clarity that you need comes when you tie together your values and your purpose. Having clarity within your goals attaches you to them on a deeper level. They are connected to your identity.

The feeling of being unsure of where you're going or why you're going there is unsettling. You don't have to live in robotic mode, doing things day to day, dealing only with what's right in front of you. You deserve to know that there is a purpose within your goals. Even when you can't see exactly what step is next, you know why you are pushing forward. Check in with yourself, understand what your core values really are, and base your goals around them.

Here's something I know for sure about goals and unlocking new achievements: You absolutely will not find your path until you start walking. You might be so paralyzed by fear of the first step that if somebody offered you the option to stay where you were and take the easy way out, it's likely that you're going to choose that. But there isn't a single person that ever reached a goal, created something new, or built anything by staying still.

We get so comfortable in the uncomfortable way that we live because it's what we know. We don't know what our lives would look like if we made healthier choices, or if we chose careers where we were happy, or we walked away from relationships that hurt us. We aren't sure of what life would look like, so we don't walk toward it. We would rather continue to sit in the comfort of our discomfort because we know what that looks like.

The worst thing that happens when you make a choice, or take a step, is that you fail. You feel as if you've made the wrong choice, and then you have to sit in that discomfort. That's where you grow. That path that feels wrong holds a lesson for you. Every path you walk is for a purpose. If the path we choose to walk ends with failure, we blame ourselves for making that choice—but what lessons have we learned? Lessons are success.

I've learned my greatest lessons from my failures. In fact, those are the ones that stick with me the most. Staying where you are is not an option. Which discomfort do you want to feel: the discomfort of knowing your days will remain the same, or the discomfort of the unknown that will lead to happiness and greater days?

I have learned through working on myself and with my clients that getting overwhelmed and shutting down is one of the biggest reasons we don't achieve what we set out to do. The overwhelm of a dream that's too big tells us it was not meant for us. Pick something smaller. Walk away from that. That will be too hard. I can't tell you how many times I've heard a story of someone setting a goal only to immediately follow up the idea with an excuse of why they can't do it. I'd love to be in better shape; I just don't have the time. I would love to have my own business; it's just not realistic right now. I would love to be in a relationship where I feel heard and respected; it's probably my fault.

Do any of these sound familiar?

You have already convinced yourself that you can't complete a goal before you even try. This cycle is vicious. With any goal that's not achieved, you have two options: change the goal, or change the plan. If you want to change the goal because you don't believe in yourself, that's not a valid reason. Try again. You need a new plan, new tools, more guidance, and more accountability—all things you are capable of getting.

We keep goals, visions, or dreams that seem too big to ourselves. We tell ourselves that if we say it out loud, we might sound stupid. When the goals are too big, we immediately put it under the category of being unachievable. Again, we convince ourselves that we can't do it before we even start. We might stare at it for a little bit, and after coming to the conclusion that it's going to be too hard, we decide not to start. We are back in the position of being overwhelmed—as most of us are—with our busy lives. We have the belief that we can't achieve it and the expectation that we won't.

But I want you to stop having the expectation that you're going to wake up tomorrow and do your whole life differently. You have been living for however many years on this earth, doing it the way you were doing before. Your transformation into believing in yourself enough to achieve goals isn't going to happen overnight.

Let's say you go ahead and take the step, or you're seriously considering taking the first step, but there's a little voice in your head that's telling you you're probably going to fail. The fear of failure is probably the biggest reason people don't reach their goals. Are you overwhelmed because it seems too big, or are you simply scared of what will happen if you take the step? If you take the first step, will you fall flat on your face? If you start that business, what if you fail? If you invest in yourself, what if you don't get better? These are the questions that tumble around in your mind, keeping you from even taking one step. You are so scared of the possibility of failing, you decide it's better to not try at all.

But by not trying at all, you deprive yourself of the possibility of success. You deprive yourself of the possibility of learning the lessons that would come from the failures, if you did fail. You are basing your choice off of something that isn't fact. The truth is that it's impossible to predict if you will or will not fail, but if you're not willing to take that risk on yourself, why would anyone else?

The Plan: Smaller Steps

There is one thing that I repeat consistently to almost every client: For goals that aren't being reached, the problem isn't the goal itself. The problem is your plan. You need two things to achieve a goal: first, belief in yourself, and second, a plan. It sounds simple, right?

Here's the truth: Every goal requires multiple steps. Whether it's organizing a closet or starting a new career, there are steps involved. To organize a closet, you have to go in the closet, pull the stuff out, go through the stuff, and then place what you want to keep back into the closet. A plan that's broken down into very small steps helps us break through that fear of taking the first step. It seems much less overwhelming to focus on the first step of going into the closet than just staring at the enormous goal of organizing the closet all at once.

Grab a piece of paper. If there's anything that you want to do right now, write that down at the top of the page and make a list underneath it of different steps that would be involved. There's a lot of goals that you may have that you won't know all the steps to, and that's okay. What happens when you complete a step is that the next step will become clear to you. This is the clarity that shows up as a result of believing in yourself and keeping your own promises. When you peel back one layer, the other layer will be there waiting for you, and then you have your next step.

One of the greatest advantages about breaking things into smaller chunks is the confidence it builds. The best place to start is by simply setting a goal that you actually know you're going to do. It can be in addition to something you're already doing, making it easier on yourself to actually follow through. The purpose of setting these tiny goals is to show yourself that you can do what you say you're going to do. You are creating a habit of keeping promises to yourself.

These tiny goals don't seem like much, but they build to something much bigger. Once you start to see that develop, the bigger goals (or bigger steps) seem more achievable. This builds your belief in yourself. This will also build your momentum. Once you start, and it feels really good, you will keep doing it because of how good you feel. You're excited about it most days, and even on the days where you're not excited, you do it anyway. This comes as a result of those tiny goals, of the addition of something new to something you were already doing. It's not a huge shift in what you are already doing, but what it creates is huge. You start to see that you are following through and eager to do more as well.

Clarity in Goals: Specificity

Lots of people make their goals very general. They do this subconsciously, so they have something to blame when it's not achieved. If you don't make the goal specific enough, you can use it as an excuse.

For example, let's take a common, too-vague goal: "I want to get healthy." It's so general that you can easily slide in a number of excuses. This was me. Until I defined what "healthy" meant to me and the actual actions I would take, it didn't happen. My goal of wanting to be healthy became losing fifty pounds. When you make the goal very specific, you lay out a plan that is specific. When something goes wrong, because something will always go wrong, you learn how to adapt while still being tied to the goal that is connected to your purpose.

At a certain point, you might even stop setting goals because you have no idea what you want. Or you might stop setting them because you've built the habit of not following through. This is why setting and achieving goals has to be tied to our purpose and our values. We can create a plan and put great physical action into place, but if we don't believe in our abilities to do the underlying work, we're going to be stuck in the same spot.

One of the most powerful things you can do when you are struggling to believe in yourself is create accountability. Find someone who does believe in you—their inspiration is contagious. Put yourself around people who drive you and make you want to take that first step. After they start pushing you to take steps, your confidence builds, and then you realize that you're finally keeping promises to yourself without their help.

Problems With Goals

One problem here is that, in the creation of this plan, we often have unrealistic expectations for ourselves. We expect ourselves to learn and implement new skills overnight, and when we don't do things perfectly, we quit. Another problem I see with goals frequently is that people don't manage their time well.

I need to ask you to do something for me. Please stop saying you don't have time. It's the most used excuse in the book. Yes, your calendar is full, but you are the one filling it.

The first thing I need you to do, if a lack of time is your excuse, is go ahead and head back to chapter two. Reread about seeing your value and prioritizing yourself. That's the real problem; you aren't valuing yourself enough to put your goals into your schedule. You have the time to do the things that you want to do; you just have to want something better for yourself. Managing your time is important, and if you find yourself self-sabotaging, you have to take action. You need the physical action of managing your time better as well as the underlying knowledge that you are important and valuable. You do have time. You just have to want to do the things you say you're going to do.

A final problem you may have with goals is focusing too much on what you want to do, not who you want to be. One of my top five books of all time is a book called *Atomic Habits* by James Clear. In this book, he talks about tying your visions and goals to your identity. This is exactly what I am talking about when I say to tie your goals to your values and your purpose. He teaches that when we base our goals more on the person we want to become, rather than external things we want to change, they become more long-lasting. The goal is tied to our purpose as a person. I translate this as tying it to your heart, so that on those days you feel like you don't want to take a step, you have a reason to do it anyway. It becomes more about who you want to be and less about the thing you want to change.

A good question to ask yourself if you are struggling with setting goals is: Who do you want to be?

Final Note: Routines

There is a lot of power in routine. I actually suggest morning and night routines for all of my clients. We can be creative with what we do with this time, but a routine is a great way to build the habit of keeping promises to ourselves.

Routines are habits that give you momentum. They are little habits that add up to a bigger goal. My routine includes getting into a mindset of gratitude every morning. This habit has created a completely different perspective and a more positive outlook on life.

A routine for you could be something as simple as getting up before your kids to have time for yourself. This creates a bigger impact when you start your day less stressed and overwhelmed. These routines show up for us long term because when we do little things consistently, we realize we can do big things, too.

Big goals can be scary, but if we create a plan, start small, and learn to believe in ourselves, everything becomes achievable.

How to set and achieve goals:

1. *Write them down.*

I write down every single goal that I have. Once I take something out of my head and put it on paper, it makes it feel real. I've done this for almost everything that I've achieved in my life. I write down daily, weekly, monthly, and yearly goals. Creating a visual reminder of what you are working toward is one of the most powerful things you can do. Many things we want to work on aren't going to give us instant gratification. When we see our goals regularly, it reminds us of what we are doing and why. You can create a vision board or write down the goal in a journal—with your plan, of course. Once you write the goal down, it opens your mind to the steps that might be a part of that goal, and then you can develop the plan.

2. *Make them specific.*

Have you ever heard of "SMART" goals? The first time I heard about this was actually on a call with a client, who is a teacher. We were talking about creating her individual goals, and she brought up how she could use the "SMART goal" system she teaches to her students for herself.

The acronym SMART stands for specific, measurable, attainable, relevant, and time-based. You know now why you need to make your goals specific, and this gives you an outline of how to do that. With this system, there is also accountability that won't allow you to make excuses.

3. *Break them down*.

I can't tell you the number of times I said I was going to write a book and then just didn't. I was overwhelmed with not knowing where to start. I also used the time excuse because I had two toddlers. Until I reached out for help and learned the steps necessary, I was frozen. I've touched on this time and time again, but the importance of making bigger goals into smaller steps (tiny goals!) is often overlooked. The only way I was able to write this was having the steps laid out in front of me. I then tackled just one step at a time, instead of continuing to tell myself I was going to write a book...eventually. Take your bigger goal, write the steps you know (remember, you might not know all of them), and start where you are, with what you have.

4. *Schedule them*.

When I first started going to the gym consistently, I had to plan ahead the days I wanted to go because I wasn't able to drive myself. I had lost my license after getting a second DUI. So I bought a paper planner and put in my work schedule and my gym schedule. Then I stuck to it.

When you have an appointment with the dentist or a meeting for work in your calendar, it's pretty likely you're going to show up. It sounds silly, and very simple, but appointments make us feel accountable.

Once you've broken down your goal into steps, they will require action on your part, which you should put right into your schedule. You're creating an appointment with yourself to work toward a goal. I'd say that's an important appointment.

5. *Actually do it.*

For some of you, it will take a rock bottom like mine to realize you don't have a choice. I didn't take action until I was forced to. No matter how many years you've told yourself you can't, I promise that you can. This is the hardest part to put into action. I can tell you how to write out your goals, and tips to help you achieve them, but when all is said and done, belief in yourself is what everything comes back to.

You have to want to become a person who is so tied to that goal, moving forward and achieving things for yourself feels urgent, like a necessity. I want you to think of something hard that you've been through and made it to the other side. You made it, didn't you? You walked through whatever was in front of you because you had to. And you'll do the same thing here. You'll face the first step head-on, even if you're shaky in your confidence. And you will see when you keep showing up that each time gets a little easier.

Chapter Summary:

- You don't know your path until you start walking.
- Tie your goals to your purpose, your values, and your identity.
- Clarity on your next steps for achieving a goal comes when you learn to believe in yourself.
- If you aren't reaching the goal, change the plan.

- If you are overwhelmed, break the goal down.
- If you are scared of failing, try anyway.
- You have the time; you just have to choose *you* and your goals.
- Set smaller goals to build your confidence.
- Create routines to inspire bigger change.

CHAPTER FIVE

INSTALL FOOTINGS - PHYSICAL ANCHOR

Movement, Nutrition, and Sleep

If you weren't aware, our emotional or mental struggles usually manifest physically. I'm sure you've heard of heart attacks being associated with stress, or noticed how happy you are after a great workout. How feelings manifest physically is different for every individual, but for me it was in the ever-changing weight of my body.

I started struggling with my weight in elementary school. I remember specifically what caused the spiral of shame about my appearance. First I got big, round glasses. Next up, steady weight gain in a short period of time. I topped this off with getting braces in seventh grade. Talk about a transformation! I was bullied and made fun of. I didn't feel confident about who I was internally, so I was just looking for any way I could cope.

In middle school, I finally recognized that I could have power over food. There weren't many things in my life that I had control over, so food became my way to cope. I coped by overeating, which led to a spike in weight gain. This was followed up by some disordered eating and undereating. At the start of my high school weight loss, I told myself, "If I lose weight, boys will like me." The cycle of losing and gaining weight was pretty much on repeat for many years after that.

When I was arrested, I was on the heavier side of my fluctuation. When I gave up drinking and partying, my comfort again became food. It was in the year that I was sober that I got to my heaviest weight. My physical transformation started after I had begun my mental transformation.

I always had the view that if I could get my body to look a certain way, I would be happier. I believed that if I lost weight, I would be accepted, loved, and seen. That was so far from the truth. Regardless of how I changed my body, my insides felt the same, and those feelings eventually came back to the surface. Once I recognized my own value and began respecting myself, I wanted to treat my body with more respect. I had to change my insides before I could change my outside.

My body has done remarkable things since I started working out in 2011. I lost fifty pounds and then went on to compete in figure and powerlifting competitions for three years. I won my figure pro card through a drug-tested federation and continued to compete in powerlifting. I loved the ability to make my body stronger. It was almost as if my resilience from my lessons was manifesting physically. I spent five years competing in these two sports. It felt incredible to build the mental strength and to push myself physically, and there were so many lessons in each experience. Once I felt more mentally and emotionally stable, I stopped using food to cope with my life. I was able to explore many types of food and build a better relationship with my body. Each physical milestone was proof of the internal work I had done, and continued to do.

After many years of competing, I had my son in 2016 and my daughter in 2018. Creating human life is something I am eternally grateful for.

I know that it's not an ability every woman has. Yet I had fearful thoughts about my body while pregnant. I feared the weight gain as well as the pressure of returning my body to the way it once was. I was forced to trust in myself and keep the focus on things within my control. Throughout both pregnancies, I was able to stay active and feel proud of my relationship with food. The habits I had built prior showed up for me. Installing the footings of our physical anchor gives us stability for our long-term health.

Prioritizing Health

Physical health is an important anchor for your life. I know you have struggled with your weight or your body image at some point. It's easy to place the blame on food and exercise. It's easy to blame the quick food options that are available, the amount of time you have, or the food you have access to. The way we treat our bodies, and value our health, has to be prioritized. *You* have to be the priority. In order for you to continue to live, and live fully, your health matters.

Most people don't recognize the connection between mental and physical health, even though they notice the shift in mood when they move their bodies consistently. This connection was actually what caused the shift in my business. I began in the fitness industry in 2011 while on my own fitness journey. What I realized after building relationships with thousands of women was that it wasn't really about the food and exercise. It was about how women felt about themselves and their ability to do what was necessary to achieve their goals.

This is when I started to focus on mental health. I realized that if we focus on the underlying mindset work along with taking physical action, we can reach any goal. This is when I realized that when you take the focus off trying to change your body because you hate your body, you see things differently.

When you make the shift to seeing your choices honestly, and wanting to make choices out of respect for yourself, you become more mindful of what your choices are. When you stop making choices out of self-hate, or just not feeling good about yourself, the changes become long-lasting. Once you believe *you* are important, you will understand the importance of your health.

When you wake up in the morning, how do you feel? When we move our bodies, and eat in a way that feels good to us, our bodies feel better. Being inactive for long periods makes us unhappy. If you knew that you would feel more positive, happy, or productive with consistent movement, would you make it a priority? I notice a drastic difference in my mood depending on how I start my day, and that's why I prefer to have movement as part of my morning routine. That means movement occurs during the first part of the day, regardless of how early it is. I do it even when I don't want to do it, because I know my day will go better because of it.

I want you to shift your mindset about your body. View feeding yourself well and moving your body as requirements rather than options. It's more important than showing up for a job, and I know you are showing up for your job when you don't want to. You clock in and show up to get your paycheck because you know there's a reward on the other side. The same goes for your health. You are rewarded with happiness, emotional stability, and pride in yourself.

When you take care of yourself physically, it shows up in other areas of your life as well.

While motivation isn't something that we have all the time, I do believe that we can build a consistent habit of respecting ourselves. Having respect for ourselves is a constant reminder of why we are making the choices we make, and respect creates discipline. On the days where motivation isn't present, respect and discipline will be. Go back to a time where you were consistently moving your body and feeding yourself well. Did you notice you were happier? Did you notice how you felt proud at the end of the day? When you feel good, you are happier and more fulfilled, and you treat people better.

You get one body. Once you recognize how valuable you really are, it allows space for you to build respect for yourself. When you respect yourself, you make choices that make you proud. Our bodies can change and adapt to so many things as women. Taking care of our physical health is a priority, and most of us need to do the mental work to believe that.

Nutrition

I haven't gone a day in my life, since I started coaching, without talking to a woman who is struggling with her nutrition. When I started my journey as a coach in 2011, I taught many women how to build better relationships with food. I found what most women want is something simple and easy. When nutrition gets too complicated, we get overwhelmed and shut down.

So I broke everything down to three nutritional habits. The purpose of these habits is to give you sustainable guidelines without unrealistic, restrictive expectations. I've found that when we make a choice that doesn't make us feel proud, it's usually the opposite of one of these habits.

1. ***Don't go longer than four hours without eating.***
   This nutritional habit came about after going through timing, and frequency, of meals with so many women. A common problem I saw was women going long periods without eating and then overeating when they finally did eat. Sound familiar? When you go such a long period of time without eating, you are more likely to eat whatever you can, removing the mindful choice of how much you want to eat. The problem is not snacking. The problem is eating more than you wanted to because you had been hungry for such a long period of time. Paying attention to when you eat will prevent you from getting to the point where you're so hungry you want to eat everything in sight.

2. ***Have a protein source every time you eat.***
   I'm going to keep this one simple for you: Peanut butter is not a protein source. I know, I love peanut butter, too. Protein sources are any foods that have more protein than fat and carbs according to the label. Lean meats, fish, egg whites, greek yogurt, and protein shakes (they make vegan protein powders, too!) are all within this category. Make sure that each time you eat, you have a food that is protein-dense. It will keep you full longer, and it's important for your immune system and body composition. Protein powder is a quick and easy way to get it in!

3. ***Pay attention to your portions.***
   When you're eating your meal, be mindful. You don't need to

overthink it. You don't need to have an exact plan detailing the amount you're going to eat. You just need to make an educated choice that aligns with your goals. You have the power over the food, and you can look at labels to learn more about foods. I know if you were raised in a "clean plate club" house, this will be a challenge for you. Just know that you have the power, always, to decide how much you want to eat.

Here's something I urge you to keep in mind when trying to change your nutrition: Please do not restrict yourself from any foods or any food groups. There are far too many diets out there with fancy names and marketing tactics that make you think they're superior to the last trending diet. Taking away a certain food group or pulling away certain foods creates a caloric deficit, and this deficit can result in fat loss. The problem is, restricting yourself is likely to result p in eating way more of whatever the item was at a later date. Eat foods that make you perform well and fuel your body. Eat in a way that makes you feel good.

If you were a proud member of the "clean plate club" growing up, you might struggle with thinking you have to finish everything that's in front of you. However, your health and your body will always be worth more than any meal that ends up in the trash or a to-go box. I understand that there are people less fortunate than us that can't afford the foods that we have. I know that you might feel some guilt when throwing away food, but finishing every bite doesn't make them any more fortunate or any less hungry. Take care of yourself, and prioritize your health. Don't make decisions based on trying to earn the clean plate that your grandparents wanted.

The last, and probably most important, thing that I want to cover with nutrition is that if you find yourself suffering from an eating disorder (or disordered eating), please reach out for help. It is *normal* to have this struggle. There is nothing wrong with you. You just need better tools to be able to navigate it. Therapy to build a better relationship with food is something that you will feel proud of when you take that step. Therapy of any fashion is one of the best things that you can do for your life. Understand that if you are struggling with food, there is help for you.

Movement

My favorite thing about our bodies is the way they are able to move. I'm fascinated by all the different types of movement. I have a rule for clients, and for myself, called #dailymovement. You are required to move your body for thirty minutes a day. It's simple, implementable, and attainable. It can be a walk, strength training, or a fitness class— as long as you are moving and it makes you feel good.

The purpose of daily movement is for you to build consistency and keep promises to yourself. It allows you to beat the all-or-nothing mindset that exercise has to look a certain way. Committing yourself to thirty minutes allows you to let go of the thought that you're not good enough, or your workout is not hard enough. The last thing we need is to feel like we're not enough.

Much like nutrition, don't view respecting yourself and moving your body as only an option. You must move your body. What *is* an option is *how* you move your body. It doesn't matter if you like to run, bike, lift, or swim, the important thing is that you are consistent. Movement is necessary for your mental health and physical health, and if restricting yourself to a certain type of movement prevents you from showing up, it's not the movement for you. Allow yourself flexibility with how you train, especially if you find yourself becoming bored or dissatisfied.

You want to prevent putting yourself in the situation where movement becomes only an option for you, and that means letting go of expectations that exercise should look a certain way. Committing to thirty minutes allows you to embrace the fact that when your gym is closed, you can still go for a walk outside.

When I was competing in powerlifting, there were days I didn't want to show up, but I did anyway because I wanted to compete and I had the desire to progress in that sport. When I quit competing, I had a hard time finding my purpose with movement again, especially after having each of my children. I had to work on letting go of the mindset that there was only one way I could train.

If you want to get better at a specific type of movement, you need to repeat that movement regularly. If you want to focus on building your consistency with movement, you need flexibility. Unless you are a competitor of some sort, you have the ability to be flexible and explore different types of movement.

Again, movement isn't only an option, but you choose how you move. There are benefits to all different kinds of training, but there are no benefits when you don't move at all. The best kind of movement is always going to be the kind you show up for. With the ability to explore different types of movement, you get to find out what you really enjoy.

This might look like falling in love and buying a Peloton after one spin class like me. Had I not gone out of my comfort zone and broken through my "powerlifting is the only way" mentality, I would have never taken that class.

I can't tell you how many times people have told me they just don't like working out. It's my belief they just haven't found the right type of movement yet. This is why getting out of your comfort zone is so important. Ask a friend to take a class with you, take a class online, sign up for a sport! You will never know until you try. I don't know anyone who has ever worked out and regretted it afterward. Embrace your freedom to explore different types of movement and keep the promise to just move consistently.

Sleep

Let's talk about sleep, baby! When I was starting in my transition to building a solid foundation for myself, I was also bartending. Sober. It was definitely not my first choice, but I also was lacking that clarity on what I wanted to do with my life. It was no surprise I ended up near alcohol, but it was strange on the other side of the bar.

With bartending also came late-night hours, and that meant I was working until 2 a.m. and going to bed between 3 and 4 a.m. I would roll out of bed early afternoon and go about my day. I had no bedtime routine, no established sleep habits, and I felt tired (which led to me eating more) most of the time. My energy started to build when I was working out regularly and started to feed myself well, but it wasn't until I started taking my sleep seriously that I noticed everything working together.

Maybe you stay up way too late, fall asleep with the TV on, or are staring at your phone for too many hours before bed. I'm going to spare you all of the scientific research on each of these topics, but let's just agree that you need to take your sleep seriously. Your quality of sleep matters, and these are all things that affect how quality your sleep really is.

I know when your kids go to bed you want to catch up on your favorite shows. I know that when the day is done you want to check out and stare at a screen. I feel you. With two toddlers, my brain is dead by 7 p.m. But I know for a fact I have more energy and can be more productive because I have a solid bedtime routine and sleep environment. I sleep an average of eight hours a night. (Sorry, moms of newborns. You'll get your sleep back soon!)

I am a big believer in morning and night routines. A night routine is like any other plan that sets you up for success, you are showing your brain that it's time to calm down and get ready to recover. If you expect that you could go from being at a concert with lights, music, and dancing to being asleep ten minutes later, you are crazy. Why do you expect to stare at your phone until your eyes hurt and then drift peacefully off to sleep? You have to wind down. You need repeated habits so your brain knows it's time to sleep.

If you don't have a nightly routine already, my suggestion is to start small. Try putting your phone away fifteen minutes before you go to bed. Wash your face and brush your teeth. Just putting your phone away and not laying in bed on your phone, over time, will make a difference. You will notice that you fall asleep quicker, too. Once you have your quick bedtime routine down, you can try adding in reading or journaling. I have a read every night rule, even if it's one page. If you fall asleep with the TV on or sleep with it on all night, I want you to stop. Take the TV out of your room if you need to. Whatever the type of screen, remove it before your bedtime routine.

I know that you understand sleep is important, but I really want you to recognize how much of a necessity it is, and how many areas of your life it affects. Sleep is the time when our brains recover and recharge, which means that if we aren't getting that recovery and recharging, we aren't functioning at our best. Without good sleep, you will be more emotionally reactive and less productive.

While working with my clients, I also noticed the link between overeating and lack of sleep. Our brains are simply looking for energy to stay awake, and for us, that translates to food. For many of you, the hunger that you are feeling could be from lack of sleep. Living in a chronic state of fatigue holds you back from accomplishing things. With better sleep, you have more clarity. More clarity means you can be more productive, and being more productive means you are reaching goals you've set.

Once I finally quit my bartending job, I went from sleeping about six hours a night to sleeping eight-plus hours. Even during my transition into motherhood with two babies, I've prioritized sleep for them and for myself. Just like movement, I don't look at my night routine or my sleep hours as optional. I can have flexibility for special events, of course, but I contribute much of my health and accomplishments to getting quality sleep. If you are sleeping six hours a night, work toward seven. And commit to showing up to your bed without your phone, consistently.

If you want to feel better physically, I want you to follow these five steps:

1. *Practice the three nutritional habits.*
    I've restricted foods and starved myself. It didn't work for long periods of time. Simplify your nutrition, eat foods that make you feel proud, and fuel your body. Don't go more than four hours without eating. Make sure there is protein in each of your meals. And pay attention to the portions that you're eating. If you break one of these habits, be kind to yourself and try again next time.

2. *#dailymovement*
    Let go of the all-or-nothing mindset. Movement is a necessity, but you have flexibility in how you move. Move your body every day for thirty minutes, and focus on being consistent. Explore different types of movement, and remember that the best type of exercise is the kind you show up for consistently.

3. *Sleep an average of eight hours.*
    Be strict with your nighttime routine and get rid of screens before bed. Honor and respect your sleep times. Put them in your schedule if you need to. IPhone even has an alarm that will alert you fifteen minutes before your bedtime! Use whatever tools you need to in order to plan for success. Set up a nightly routine that allows you to wind down before sleep.

4. *Make doctor's appointments ahead of time.*

Don't wait until something is wrong to get checkups from the doctor. The best way to do this is to make your next appointment when you are there. Get your yearly exams and regular cleanings. Especially when it comes to the dentist, checkups and cleanings are small and easy appointments, but they are necessary. Valuing your health is part of loving yourself, and these appointments are easy to let slide to the back burner.

Chapter Summary:

- There is a connection between our mental and physical health. You have to do the work on both ends.
- Feeding yourself well is part of respecting yourself. You must believe it is worth feeling proud of your food choices.
- When you take care of your physical health, your life gets better.
- You have *one* body. Take care of it.
- Don't restrict foods or food groups. Set yourself up for success by having a reasonable, healthy plan.
- Your "clean plate club" membership has been revoked. Prioritize yourself over your plate.
- If you suffer from an eating disorder (or disordered eating), seek therapy.
- Move your body for thirty minutes a day.
- Movement isn't only an option; the type of movement is.
- Explore different types of movement.
- Create a nighttime routine.
- Remove screens before bed.
- You can accomplish more with consistent quality sleep.

CHAPTER SIX

INSTALL FOOTINGS -
INTELLECTUAL ANCHOR

Building Knowledge and Confidence

There isn't a day that goes by that I'm not impressed by my husband's knowledge. The man is a human Wikipedia. Just don't ask him to remember something from the grocery store without a list—yikes.

Playing any sort of trivia game with him is, honestly, not very fun. In the beginning of our relationship, I would stay silent because I didn't feel I could bring any value to conversations over topics I didn't know much about. There were even certain points in our relationship where we would be having conversations (or playing trivia games) and I would start to beat myself up a little because I felt stupid.

I was in gifted classes throughout middle school and some of high school before I started my trek down a darker path. I actually enjoyed school and really liked learning. Math and any sort of equations were my jam.

When I fell out of love with learning, it was because I was filling my time with entertaining boys and spending my mental energy figuring out when the next party would be. I completely derailed from something I enjoyed because I didn't feel good about myself. Funny how that works, eh?

I didn't have any standard to hold myself to, so I committed to the bare minimum with school and focused on trying to find fulfillment in drinking and exploring ways to numb myself. It was a natural pull, away from any sort of learning or knowledge.

When I feel like I could not contribute or add value to a conversation due to my perceived lack of education or knowledge, I feel less valuable. When I first started dating Eric, I felt less confident, and like I wanted to crawl into a hole, because I felt like I didn't bring any value to some of our conversations.

As I continued to build my business and refine my craft, I realized that it wasn't about comparing intelligence or who knows more facts in general. It wasn't about how much information I retained or if I could win trivia. It was about how confident I felt.

I had unrealistic expectations for thinking I should retain facts about things I didn't put time or genuine effort into learning. We all have passions for different areas, and those passions drive us to learn more.

I've always been interested in why we do the things that we do. I've always wanted to get to the root of what's going on—and fix it. I always want to know more about myself and how I could become better. Self-discovery is fascinating to me, while history is not, and of course, I retain knowledge in the areas I have passion for.

When I started to gain knowledge in new areas, I noticed that I was more confident in similar situations. Since committing my time to learning about things that help me to be a better human, coach, mother, and wife, I feel more knowledgeable and confident. I still may not have the trivia knowledge that Eric has, but I always have something to contribute that I feel is valuable enough.

If I feel ignorant about a situation, I can't blame others for knowing more about that topic than me. I have to take responsibility for not taking the initiative to learn. What I realize is that the more I learn about the things that I'm passionate about, the more I can help others. The more I learn about myself, the more I can help others. While Eric will likely forever beat me in trivia games, I never have to feel like I am worth less because we just have different skills and interests. Furthermore, if I am frustrated or not feeling confident, I can choose to educate myself.

One of the biggest goals I hear from clients is a desire to gain confidence in themselves. You might not recognize how much your confidence is linked to your knowledge. When I think about the times I've stayed silent, it's because I didn't know what to say, and I didn't feel empowered enough to speak up. I'm not just talking about math and history here; I'm talking about self-knowledge. It is not so much a lack of confidence, but the fear of others' judgement if you show them your real self.

If you feel confident and educated about who you are, you can stop beating yourself up about not knowing enough. You can learn to speak up. You can take the time to build knowledge through self-discovery, and then you will feel more confident in every situation. Installing the footing of our intellectual anchor allows consistent growth that stabilizes us and inspires us to continue to grow.

Gaining Confidence - Gaining Knowledge

I believe we can build our confidence in many different ways, and when you combine your knowledge and passion for something is likely when you're going to feel the most confident. You can read, write, talk, take classes, listen to podcasts—the options are endless. You just have to want to learn more and be confident in your ability to show up.

If you were to ask me to walk into a room and teach a history class, I would probably shit my pants (damn, I hope none of my history teachers are reading this). You can't have the expectation to show up without fear in situations you know nothing about. If you think you are going to waltz into a first class xand not feel like you are going to puke a little, you might be crazy. Here, again, you have the opportunity to focus on just showing up, even if you feel ignorant, nervous, or worth less than others. Most times, the more you know, the more confident you will be. The combination of drive and passion that helps get you through the discomfort of learning is what causes growth.

Learning more about yourself, or anything that you are passionate about, will bring you comfort. If I were asked to teach that same history class, after being given a guideline of what I'm teaching, what to say, and what questions to ask, I'd be golden. I would still have fear going into the situation because it's still something new, but with that little bit of knowledge, I'd be able to at least show up with an idea of what I was going to do. I'd be able to at least feel a little more comfortable in the situation knowing I had some bullet points to follow, rather than just trying to wing it.

The more you learn about yourself, the more empowered you become. The more empowered you are, the more your goals get accomplished. The more your goals get accomplished, the more confident you become. The more confident you are, the more fulfilled you feel. This is why the intellectual anchor is so important. It's not about just reading books or signing up for courses. It's about following whatever path you are passionate about, and making a promise to yourself to evolve and grow.

Finding Your Passion

The empowerment that comes with knowing who you are, what you enjoy, where you are going, and what you want to do is untouchable. Knowing your values and basing your continuing education on things that align with who you are makes you more likely to reach the next level. In order to get to a place of confidence within yourself, you have to explore new paths and expand your skills.

You are likely thinking along the lines of formal education when you think of an intellectual anchor. It certainly can be school, a new career path, or some sort of formal education—if that aligns with who you are and where you want to go. However, the key here is you have to start small, just like any other goal. Starting small can mean exploring something around that interest. If you value health, you can explore fitness classes that could lead to fitness coaching.

If you've ever had a sparked interest in something and then rushed to your phone to search Google about it, that's gaining knowledge. You can take it a step further and read a book, go to a class, or take a course. You don't necessarily have to jump into a college class to gain knowledge. Having consistent learning—however informal—in your life allows you to become more confident, as you are expanding or learning new skills. Along that journey, you can even find your true purpose.

Had I not started bringing friends with me to the gym to show them what I was doing, I wouldn't have found my love for fitness which led to my love for personal development. It starts with a spark. If you think about a skill that you value, you can likely remember the spark that led to the love of that skill. Pure curiosity can cause us to dive in deeper. We feel ignited and fueled by new information. We are wired to continue learning. You have to follow that curiosity or that passion and just take one step, read one book, find one mentor, or take one class that lets you tap into that wealth of knowledge.

Managing Expectations

We can completely alter the way that we look at building confidence by just committing to showing up. That's it. I need you to stop expecting yourself to be the best at everything right when you start.

At thirty-two years old, I walked into my first hip hop dance class. I was scared shitless. Surrounded by eight other people in which the average age was seventeen, I felt like an idiot. This was before we started dancing. I lack coordination, and when I say that, I mean it in the kindest way toward myself—but seriously, it's bad. Throughout the class, I was so frustrated and embarrassed. I couldn't believe how awful I was. In my head, I had seen myself dancing with the best of them after an hour or two, but that was apparently not going to be the case.

After the class, I sat in my car and told myself, "Kelsea, did you really go in there expecting to pop, lock, and drop it like the Instagram videos you watch? You've never danced, much less danced hip hop—unless you want to count the drunken bumping and grinding in the half-conscious state you were accustomed to."

I had an unrealistic expectation. I know it's hard when you have perfectionist blood running through your veins. Here's the truth, though; Perfect is a lie. It doesn't exist. There is no such thing, and reaching for it sets you up to fail.

I showed up to that dance class, and I wasn't good at the beginning. But I showed up and I had to be proud of myself for that. If I had given into my frustration and allowed myself to fall into the trap of high expectation, I wouldn't have continued to explore the possibility of improving at all.

Again, the only expectation I want you to have when you start something new is to just show up. Commit to just being there and taking in the knowledge the experience will give you. Committing to something new and showing up will build your confidence. At the end of the day, you get to say, "I went there. I did that. I showed up." Even if you have the coordination of a baby giraffe. Have the expectation that when you start something new, you aren't going to be very good. Reflect and reward yourself for simply putting yourself in that new position, and love yourself for being brave. Continuing to put yourself in environments that may feel uncomfortable will make you believe that you can do anything.

You know now that pursuing consistent learning in some way, making the commitment to just show up, and allowing yourself to explore are the ways to increase your confidence. This won't happen if you stay in your comfort zone. Wherever you are right now, it's likely there is something you want to change, or something you want to be better at, but there are underlying fears holding you back. You have excuses that you're not ready to address, even if the excuses seem valid.

It's easy to allow ourselves to make these excuses. You tell yourself you can't possibly take that step until your kids are older, you can't start that business until you have more time. I've heard it all. You are comfortable with the discomfort of your life. You have to take a small step, one that is right outside your comfort zone, teetering on the edge of comfort. You need to do something that's a little uncomfortable, because you're not building any confidence staying where you are.

To address your fears about stepping outside of your comfort zone, you need to ask yourself if the feelings, fears, or stories you tell yourself are even valid. If you think that you will walk into somewhere new and everybody will turn around and laugh at you because that's what happened in third grade, you have to let that go. It's highly unlikely that's going to happen when you're thirty. If you are scared of starting because you think you'll fail, what would happen if you don't even start?

You can convince yourself of anything—and make excuses based on fears from your past. This is why having the expectation that you aren't going to be very good at first is important. Anybody that is great at something now started where you are.

Think of somebody that you know that is very confident. What do they do? How do they carry themselves? How did they build their skill set? Once you know these things, you can become them. If you see it in someone else, you have the ability within you. When I think of a confident person, I picture someone that walks into rooms with their head held high. I see confidence as sitting down at tables you might be scared you don't have a place at yet. You can practice small actions like being able to say hello to someone first, or making eye contact when you walk into a room full of people.

Remember, there is always physical action you must take and underlying work you must do. The physical action is to put yourself in situations that might seem uncomfortable, to commit to showing up, to take the step. The underlying issue is to address the fears, excuses, and stories you're telling yourself. You are in control, and you have the option to write a new story.

The stories that you tell yourself are usually related to something that's happened in the past. It is what a parent told you when you were young. It is the hurtful comment someone said during an argument. You tell yourself these stories over and over again until they become your identity. You become the story because you believe the story.

Playing these old stories on repeat in your head is one of the biggest things that will block you from building confidence. You accept these stories as fact, when in reality they are usually based on one occurrence. In order to build confidence, and excel in any situation, these stories have to be worked through and questioned. Once you work through these stories, you will be able to write a new one.

You're not going to put yourself in new situations to explore or commit to the promise of showing up when you don't believe you are worth it. I know that you want to feel more confident, and it's likely that you have some confidence in certain areas already. Examine those areas. What led you to being able to show up confidently? You can take your confidence from other areas and apply it to the areas where you feel less confident.

How to build this intellectual anchor for your foundation:

1. *Read.*

When I was little, my grammy would take me to the local library in Hurst, Texas, every time I stayed with her. I would leave with stacks of *Nancy Drew* books, spending the remainder of the day lying on her couch devouring the stories. I lost my love for reading when my life was full of too many distractions. I was pulled away from the things that fulfilled me.

No matter what kind of reading you do, it expands your knowledge. You are expanding in your creativity, your vision, and your tools when you pick up a book. Never have I finished a book and not felt either fulfilled, excited, or like I had gained a new piece of knowledge. Go back and apply the goal-setting tools that we talked about and start with one book a month.

2. *Be around people who are where you want to be.*

I definitely enjoy feeling like I am the smartest person in the room. I'm sure this feeling isn't uncommon. Feeling like you can contribute increases confidence. Only putting yourself in situations where you know everything keeps you from growing. You are missing opportunities to become better.

When I felt ignorant around Eric, I wasn't confident. I felt uncomfortable. This discomfort helped me recognize that I have my own unique skill set, and it made me want to improve. Putting yourself around people who are further along in your area, have lived longer, been through different experiences, or who can teach you something is beneficial for both parties. You get to learn from their skills and the experiences that they've had, and they get to give back by using their experiences to teach you.

3. *Teach and share what you know.*

I get legitimately excited about sharing new information I have learned. Along the way, I've had great mentors and people that I've learned from. I continue to add those people in my life. I start with learning, and then my confidence grows with the new knowledge. I put my new skills into practice for myself and get to dive deeper into the experience. After I've learned and practiced new skills and seen the advantages, I can't help but want to share.

Sharing experiences with others that relates to their lives helps to create change. All of us have an area we don't feel confident in. If we learn tools or skills that help us in that area, then we feel fulfilled. Once we are fulfilled, we are able to reach out and share that with other people.

4. *Try new things.*

Anything I've gotten better at, or had success with, was the result of putting myself in an environment where I could get better. Any situation where I've excelled has required me showing up to do the work, and showing up is always the hardest part. I didn't want to show up to the gym at 5 a.m. to train someone for seven dollars. I didn't want to call in every morning to see if I was on deck to be drug tested that day. I didn't want to go to therapy appointments. You have to put yourself in uncomfortable positions and continue to try new things.

At the end of the day, you're building the confidence in your ability to show up. You are becoming someone who keeps their word. You are building trust with yourself. When you become someone that consistently shows up and does the things that you say you're going to do, you're likely to continue that pattern when things get hard. Trying new things allows you to put yourself in a position over and over again to prove to yourself you can withstand and survive discomfort.

5. *Check your stories.*

One of the biggest things that held me back was me telling myself I couldn't move forward. My mind was filled with negative stories from my childhood and many years of neglecting myself. All I wanted was to numb myself, so when I got the urge to make a change, I immediately had excuses. It was my own stories telling me that I shouldn't even try. There was no truth to those stories, but I accepted them as fact. How did I know if I was capable of changing if I had never tried before? You have to check in and ask yourself, "Is this actually true?"

Think about any story you've ever read. There's transition and change throughout the story. Characters grow, learn, and change. They go through some tribulations and learn lessons from them. You are no different. You have experiences that you walk through. You hold on to stories that play over and over again in your mind. The truth is, you're holding yourself back with the old stories. Remember, you have the ability to write new ones.

Chapter Summary:

- Fear of being who you truly are stops you from confidently showing up.
- You can rebuild trust with yourself by consistently showing up and acquiring knowledge.
- Continued growth is uncomfortable, but the knowledge you build adds confidence.
- Start small—one page of a book, one new class.
- Simply showing up builds your confidence.
- Your environment matters. Put yourself around people who inspire you.
- There is comfort within your discomfort. Staying in the comfort zone holds you back.
- Check your stories for facts. Are they valid?
- Stay curious and interested in continuous learning.
- There is empowerment that comes with new knowledge. You can lead and teach others.

CHAPTER SEVEN

INSTALL FOOTINGS - EMOTIONAL ANCHOR

Creating Stability and Security

I'm not really sure what it's like to remember a place as your "childhood home." My memories are from many different houses because my parents divorced when I was two years old. I don't recall feeling as if I ever really belonged in any certain home or space.

I saw many new relationships form and end, some shorter than others. There were many children—some I called siblings for a short period of time—that came and went. I was in a variety of environments, I had many caregivers, and what I became accustomed to was a life without structure.

The lack of stability that I remember as a child didn't faze me (or so I told myself). It was just the way my life was, and I accepted it. I thought it was normal. I tried my best to exercise any choices I did have, wanting more structure one minute and then less discipline the next.

Control makes us feel stable. It gives us a checkpoint where we recognize that we're okay. Lack of stability in our lives can cause us to lose focus, and even manifest anxiety or depression. We, as humans, are wired for connection and attention. We want to feel needed and to know what's coming next.

Did my original step on the dark path come as a result of needing attention? Possibly.

Did it get the desired result? Absolutely not.

Did it allow me to escape a life I wasn't happy in? You bet.

Many of you will minimize things that happened in childhood. You will dismiss how you felt about experiences because you don't qualify them as "traumatic." You might have the misconception that your dad saying one hurtful thing isn't a big deal. You can downplay experiences because someone else may have gone through something you feel is worse. You might think that because you are alive, healthy, and happy now, none of your past matters.

When owning our stories, we bring all these things to the surface. We accept that we were hurt, that we are holding that hurt, and once we acknowledge it, we can forgive it.

There is no perfect childhood. There is no perfect parent. The lack of stability I felt in my younger years continued into my teenage years. I didn't feel secure with my life, myself, or any of the relationships around me. Until I went through the process of self-discovery, I was unable to make the link between not feeling secure and making the choices that I was making.

Once I acknowledged the fact that my life experiences and the things that I went through were traumatic to me, and stopped normalizing them, it allowed me to forgive and move forward. That was step one: I recognized that I went through it, but I still had work to do to be able to piece together why I did the things I did.

Therapy opened all of that up for me. It allowed me to make those connections, to see why I was choosing the things (and people) that I was. What I had been shown, and the habits that I had been creating, were all a part of my learned behaviors. The most powerful part of bringing awareness to these links was that I was finally able to make different choices and create stability and security for myself. Beyond that, I got a chance to do things differently, and my hope was to create the security I was missing with my own children.

Installing the footing of our emotional anchor allows us to create structure that we may not have been aware was possible.

Acceptance

My belief, from my own experience, is that you must look at your past experiences and be accepting of the emotions that come with those experiences in order to move forward. Owning your story is that acceptance that is needed to have the room for change.

Your emotional anchor is all of the emotions you feel—the wide range that you feel each day—and how you cope with those emotions. You use your skills to navigate through emotions and create stability within your life. Our emotional anchor is a call to action to acknowledge and question our emotions. How you cope with your emotions will depend on things like learned behaviors and what the emotion is. For some, it will be the need to numb, and for others, it will be an excitement that manifests in anxiety.

There are many emotions that you likely have the habit of suppressing. In the generations before mine, talking about feelings or the importance of communication wasn't addressed. If you are sad, you are told not to cry. If you are mad, you hold it in. If you don't feel good about yourself, you fake it. And you most definitely don't ask for help, because that would be seen as weakness. Something is wrong with you if you aren't able to handle it yourself. Does this sound familiar?

Let me clear this up for you: Nothing is wrong with you. What's wrong is being taught not to speak about how you feel, or being told that your feelings aren't valid. Everything you feel is valid. Suppressing your emotions causes anger, depression, resentment, and anxiety, making you feel as if you are broken.

One of the greatest things you can do to feel more stable in your life is to accept any emotion that arises. Emotions are messages. Listen to them. Ask them questions. Let yourself feel. Security is freedom from danger or threats. If you aren't listening to your emotions, you will forever be a threat to yourself.

For many of you, acceptance is related to complacency, and so it's something you avoid. You tell yourself you're happy where you are so you can shut down and not have to try anymore. This isn't actually accepting yourself. True acceptance means being okay with where you are while understanding that you are built to grow. You can accept yourself fully as you are without blocking the potential for your own growth. Acceptance is a required step, much like acknowledgement of our feelings, in order to move forward.

Developing Stability

When you accept yourself and your emotions fully, you become open to feeling more secure. Stability is created when we can trust ourselves, when we keep promises to ourselves, and when we feel secure in knowing our feelings are sound.

As children, security is simple. We need love, attention, and care. As adults, we still require the same things. Often, we're looking outward for these things and neglecting the fact that we can also give them to ourselves. You may think that stability is created from someone else, but until you provide yourself with stability, you can't expect to receive it from others.

One of the biggest causes of anxiety is not knowing what's next, that fear of the unknown that keeps you up at night. On the other hand, knowing what will come next provides comfort. If I were to tell you that you can create a roadmap, plan, or vision that allows you to see what's next, would you believe me? It's unrealistic to plan every second of your life—flexibility in all things is important—but consistently not knowing what your day will look like is a recipe for disaster. You can create a plan, you can map out steps, or you can set up a routine to provide yourself with stability. You have to learn to turn inward, hear those feelings, and create something from them.

Now, there is the creation of a plan, and there is the implementation of the plan. Creation, for most, is easy. This is when you say you are starting something new, you research new classes to try, you lay out your clothes the night before, you write down steps one through five of how to reach a new goal.

Implementation is the difficult part, and also the most important. To make sure we are developing stability, structure, and security, we have to follow through. You have probably fallen short with implementation because you aren't secure enough in yourself and your ability to keep showing up. If you want to feel secure, you have to create that stability first. You have to show up for yourself and honor your emotions. You have the power of creating security for yourself.

You have the power to make better choices, and only you know what that better choice is. You can't forever rely on everyone else telling you what to do. It pulls you away from trusting yourself. It serves as a distraction, an excuse for not facing the feelings you are scared to acknowledge. When you take yourself back and look at the big picture of where you are, do you have a plan? What do you want to create? What checkpoints do you have in your life providing you stability?

Understanding how you cope with different emotions is a very important piece of this process. Some of you might choose drugs and alcohol like I did. Some of you might reach for that glass or two of wine every night just to block out the day. Maybe your coping mechanism is to completely throw yourself into your work as a distraction so you don't have to face your life at home. We all have areas that we ignore, suppress, or avoid, and what we do to cope is usually dependent on what the emotion is. We are so locked into getting instant gratification that we don't even question our emotions. We accept them as fact and turn them away like they don't deserve the attention they need, the attention *you* need.

When you feel unstable or insecure, you reach for comfort, and what the form of comfort is will vary. The surface-level emotions—emotional eating, outbursts of anger, et cetera—are never the first emotions. In other words, they are symptoms of a deeper emotion, like loneliness or pain. These are messages for you to dig deeper. You have the power to learn new ways to cope that align with who you are and who you want to be. It requires work that most people don't want to do, peeling back the layers under the surface. But I ask you to question the surface-level emotions you feel. Ask yourself what's been lying dormant underneath.

Applying the same technique we talked about with confidence, are there areas of your life that you do feel stable? You can take those areas and dig in, pulling out the things that have helped you build the trust there. When you are with that person or in that space, what is it that makes you feel secure? Once you recognize them, you can make it a point to implement them in the areas in which you are feeling instability. If your home life feels safe and structured because you have a great family calendar and plan for everyone, but your work feels like chaos, can you bring that scheduling to work?

Just like we talked about in the intellectual anchor, you can build knowledge in any area where you feel like you're crumbling. You can turn inward and apply what you already know to create stability in the areas where you feel like you are falling short. It requires you to stop ignoring feelings and start questioning them. Instead of thinking, "I am sad. I need to numb," you can think, "I am sad. Why? I need comfort. What brings me comfort?"

This requires that you sit in feelings instead of instantly reaching for something to take them away. It may be uncomfortable, but like stepping out of your comfort zone, it will lead to growth and long-term happiness.

You have the ability to create what feels secure to you, and when you commit to showing up for yourself, it becomes a possibility.

I want to offer you two tools that are powerful for linking emotions. They will help you move through the process of acceptance and allow for you to feel stable. The first one is knowing your values, and the second one is uncovering your learned behaviors from childhood.

Understanding your personal values will give you guidelines to help you choose what's important to you. When you make choices or decide to cope in a way that doesn't align with your values, you feel that physically. You can examine your feelings and check that they align with your values to better understand where those feelings come from. If one of your values is freedom, and you are consistently told to travel more for work, or work more hours, you may feel like you're suffocating. The restriction of that schedule doesn't align with what you actually want. Once you recognize this isn't something you want for yourself, you can do something about it. To feel stable and secure with who you are, making the effort to understand your values is one of the most powerful things you can do. When you know who you are, you can *be* who you are.

Examining your childhood, especially with a therapist, is a very eye-opening experience. Pulling out those boxes you've hidden away, hoping they would disappear, can be heart-wrenching. But doing this allows you to make connections and have a better understanding of yourself. It's easy to beat yourself up for a behavior you repeat—until you know where it comes from and why you do it. When you get to open those boxes and understand why you make the choices that you make, you finally get to feel like you have power over your life. Uncovering old thoughts allows you to start the process of writing something new. You become more secure in who you are, and you see that you can create stability for yourself.

When you recognize that you have habits that were instilled in you at a young age, it allows you to forgive yourself. And if you can forgive yourself, you can build trust with yourself again. You can stop beating yourself up for making poor choices, because those choices were all you knew. Understanding that I was replicating what I learned as a child was one of the things that allowed me to forgive myself.

Knowing your values and understanding where you came from and why you make the choices that you make is empowering. It's like finally finishing a project with numerous issues. You get to the end, and then you can understand why the piece didn't fit, why the color was wrong, and how the placement could be off. By knowing yourself, you see that you have the power to create security in your life.

When you don't feel secure in a situation, it can manifest in overreactions or anxiety. We are so quick to judge ourselves, or place blame on others, for our present situation. We react quickly when we are triggered. When you feel unsure of what tomorrow brings, it's hard to feel any sort of stability. When you wake up not knowing what your day holds, how can you expect yourself to be fulfilled and know that you are keeping in line with your values?

When you understand yourself, your values, and your triggers, you can recognize them and be more preventative moving forward. When you are aware of what bothers you and why, you can notice when you are overreacting. This stops you from judging yourself and allows you to link your reaction back to a learned behavior or misalignment of your values. When you stop bullying yourself, you can build a better plan for how you want to react in the future, or make sure you don't get to that place again.

Breaking the cycle requires compassion. We're compassionate by seeking to understand and forgiving rather than judging. Overreacting or a triggered response is a sign of something below the surface that needs to be addressed, and we have to dig deeper to gather more information and fully understand.

Being confident in who you are requires knowing who you are. Every feeling is valid. You don't need to suppress any emotion. You are allowed to feel whatever you need to feel. And you can question any feeling by taking a pause instead of reacting immediately. Taking that pause and thinking through the feeling will bring stability.

The learned behaviors of suppressing feelings and not communicating are two of the most popular subjects among my clients. Living in a household in which feelings aren't addressed results in insecurity. Many of us are taught that expressing emotions is weakness. Connecting your feelings with what you know about yourself is strength. Relearning your ability to process feelings is power. Suppression will manifest and make us feel insecure. Releasing and communicating brings stability. Luckily, times are changing, and people are realizing the power of expressing emotions. Asking for help is being more widely accepted. What a change we would have seen in the world if our parents, and grandparents, had felt the same way many years ago.

How to feel more emotionally stable and secure in your life:

1. *Acknowledge the instability and insecurity.*

The first step is always awareness. My first step was waking up in that jail cell and realizing I didn't want to live that way anymore. Without acknowledging where I was and that I wanted to live differently, I wouldn't have created a life that feels stable. Taking note of where you are and what makes you feel insecure or unstable gives you the power to move forward. You can stop suppressing or distracting and be aware of where change is required.

2. *Create structure within your control.*

I am definitely a person who fears a loss of control. I don't think there's anyone that enjoys feeling out of control, but it's also common for people to wake up realizing they're already there, unsure of how it happened. Separate the areas of your life, and look at the places that you feel are unstable. Then ask yourself, "What can I do to create some sort of structure in this space?" There are parts of every environment that are within your control. You can't control other people, but you can always control your reactions to those people. That's why you create your own structure and set boundaries, rather than forever depending on somebody to make you feel secure. You can outline a better schedule for your day-to-day living, or you can create a morning/nightly routine that gives you a sense of knowing what will happen during your day/night.

3. *Link your coping mechanisms.*

As I said, this is one of the greatest things I learned in therapy. Why do I do things that I do? Once I had that better understanding of why I was making the choices that I made, it allowed me to see that I had the power to choose differently. I encourage you to reach out and hire someone who can help you to understand more about your learned behaviors. Once you make those links, you will understand why you react or cope the way you do. For me, the lack of structure and stability, along with feeling like I didn't have control, led me to repeat behaviors that mimicked that loss of control. Find out who you are, and why you do what you do.

4. *Ask for help.*

This is a tool that can be applied to almost every situation. The truth is that none of my successes were achieved completely on my own. It always required the help of someone else. In order for me to work on this book, my husband had to be with my kids. In order for me to grow an understanding of myself and my purpose, I had to have mentors and therapy. There is no shame in needing guidance to get clarity in your life.

5. *Know your values.*

I talk to clients every single day who are feeling lost and unsure of who they are, what they want, and where they're going. After determining their values, they understand who they are and who they want to be. This allowed them to create stability. Knowing your values allows you to build a better understanding of yourself and gives you a filter to use for all of your decisions. Making choices that align with your values gives you stability.

Chapter Summary:

- We feel secure when we know what's coming next.
- You can create stability even if it wasn't learned in childhood.
- We all have areas in which we feel unstable.
- Staying connected to your values keeps you secure.
- Recognize your triggers and work through them.
- Without stability, we overreact and suppress feelings.
- Insecurity in ourselves shows up in all relationships.
- There are no inappropriate feelings. All feelings need to be acknowledged.

CHAPTER EIGHT

INSTALL FOOTINGS - SOCIAL HEALTH

Setting Boundaries and Exploring

There's no one-size-fits-all when it comes to your social life. For a long time, I was wrapped up in the thought that I needed to have this big circle of friends in order to be healthy socially. It would cause me stress as I tried to force friendships, especially when I was simultaneously trying to save friendships that had taken different paths. I was always more focused on making more friends than I was on creating quality friendships. That shift was a difficult shift for me.

Going from being the party girl who knew so many people to someone who didn't really have many friends was hard, even though it meant those few friends I did have were high-quality, wonderful friendships. I always had the perspective that if you have more friends, you must be better because more people like you. That way of thinking led to me being whoever I needed to be in order to please other people. I created many friendships in which there was no respect or loyalty because I didn't offer those things to myself.

I can remember sitting in my room after being bailed out of jail for the third time. I had the realization that I needed to change my life, and I knew that it would require changing my environment. I sobbed uncontrollably—not because of all the legal trouble that I was in, but because I recognized that I was going to have to walk away from most of the people I called friends.

Who would I be without alcohol? What would make people like me? My identity was based around my social calendar—but, even though I was always out drinking with people, I still felt alone. My priorities each day were where I was drinking and who I was drinking with. The thought of taking that away was terrifying. Now that I am more secure in who I am, and where I'm going, I don't need a big circle of friends. I don't seek or require approval from anyone. What I need is to approve of myself, and to continue to expose myself to things that allow me to grow and learn.

When we know more about ourselves, just like understanding our values, we can make better choices. Each of us requires a different amount of social activity, and so there are no right choices. The only requirement is that you feel fulfilled in this area and that you have genuine relationships that add to your life. It is important that you are valuing yourself enough to choose relationships that align with who you are and where you're going instead of seeking the approval of others. You have to find your own balance of social activity; nobody can tell you what's the best amount of interaction for you. Installing the footing of your social anchor allows you to feel proud of who you are by being in charge of your boundaries and the environments you explore.

Setting Boundaries

For many, the hardest struggle is setting boundaries within relationships. Most people view setting boundaries as creating controversy. It's not a conversation they look forward to having. What happens if you don't set boundaries is you will be overwhelmed. This will lead to burnout or emotional explosions you regret later.

For instance, an important perspective switch is to recognize that when you say yes to everyone, you're saying no to yourself. Setting boundaries teaches others how we want to be treated. I have had a number of conversations with people who are appalled at how they are being treated, and my first question is always, "Have you asked them to treat you differently?"

You might have no problem setting boundaries with other people, but you also need to have boundaries for yourself. This is what we call honoring and respecting ourselves. If you wouldn't treat someone a certain way, you need to make sure you aren't doing the same thing to yourself. You can't expect to have successful relationships with anyone until you build one with yourself.

Time management is a form of boundary that people don't even recognize. You may fill your calendar full of activities with other people, not leaving any space for yourself. The truth is that you're in charge of your calendar. Working 9 a.m. to 5 p.m.? You signed the contract. Watching your sister's kids for the third weekend in a row? You said yes. You either aren't communicating your boundaries, or you are communicating them and not holding them.

This is how overwhelm occurs; we fear disappointing others, so we continue to pile on tasks to make others happy. You might even end up playing the victim, talking about everything that you do for everybody else, wondering why nobody does anything for you.

Nobody does anything for you because you are too busy doing everything for everybody else. You've taught others you don't need time for yourself, and they are honoring that. It is your job to teach people how they can interact with you by setting your boundaries. Once you are leading by example and managing your time well, the people in your relationships will see that. Having good boundaries that reflect your values makes you more authentic. There is power in speaking up for yourself.

Whether it's in our friendship circles, our work environments, or home lives, people are only going to treat us how we allow them to treat us. It is your job to have guidelines for how someone can and cannot treat you. If you are not setting those guidelines, you can't have the expectation of someone treating you a certain way. This means you have to be honest with yourself, let go of the victim mentality, and start prioritizing yourself.

Anxiety comes from not knowing something. Not knowing feels like a loss of control. Being a part of something that we have no control over sounds terrifying, right? No matter what the situation is, there's always something that you can control. Boundaries give you control. If you live in a home with clutter that causes anxiety, clear the clutter. Communicate that the clutter is causing you anxiety, and come up with a plan on how to keep it from collecting again.

If you work in a toxic environment, where is the toxicity coming from? What can you control in that situation? You can have a conversation with a boss or co-worker to set a boundary and build a better understanding of each other. If you have communicated a boundary and it's not being respected, it's your job to honor that boundary and remove yourself from that environment. All you can do is control yourself, and part of that is communicating what your needs are. If they aren't being respected, it is your job to find them elsewhere.

If you fear controversy in communication, you can learn how to communicate in a more effective way. There's no controversy when you are expressing something that is true to yourself and speaking about how you feel. It may be scary to speak up because you think that it will cause anger or abandonment—and sometimes it does—but that isn't about you.

Like any other skill, the only way we get better is by implementing. You can't just talk about not being happy with how somebody's treating you, or the setup of a certain environment. It is your job to communicate how you will and will not be treated and what will and will not be allowed in your life. You will have to let go of the fear of disappointing others and remember to honor yourself.

Exploration

Now that you understand the importance of setting boundaries, I want to talk about another piece of the social anchor: exploration!

Exploring, or an exploration phase, is simply promising yourself to try new things. You can build confidence by showing up no matter what the activity is. As part of your exploration, you should put yourself in new situations with different types of people. You get the opportunity to meet new people, learn new skills, and do something fulfilling. Every situation will allow you to connect with, or build a better understanding of, someone else. Continuing to explore new situations will not only build your confidence, but it also can bring you clarity.

You can learn more about who you want to have in your environment and what things you enjoy.

At the very least, by trying something new, you are teaching yourself that you are a person who isn't afraid to try new things.

This past year, I signed up for a volunteer organization because I wanted to connect with others and try something new. It didn't fit into my life at the time, but I did gain a new friend, and that, to me, was well worth it. Even though it wasn't my cup of tea, I still showed up and gave it a shot. I didn't let my social anxiety win.

When you show up, you recognize you can put yourself in different (and perhaps uncomfortable) social situations with new people and still be okay. With the simple promise to yourself to just show up in an exploration phase, you are building trust with yourself and learning who you are. Consistent practice at becoming secure with yourself makes it easier.

Fear can feel like a backpack full of bricks. That shit is heavy. When you believe in yourself enough to explore new things, it builds confidence that allows you to take off that heavy backpack. The fear that's holding you back is only holding you back because you allow it to. In order to build a strong social anchor, you need to be aware and acknowledge your values, be willing to communicate and set boundaries, and also to explore and try new things. Exploration will allow you to build a better relationship with yourself and create the possibility of new opportunities.

How to build a better social anchor:

1. *Commit to an exploration phase.*

When you commit to an exploration phase, it can be one new thing a month or one thing a week, depending on your time and what you want to explore. The purpose is to actually commit and follow through. This puts you in new situations with different people and can allow you to learn new skills. At the very least, you build confidence in your ability to show up.

2. *Set environmental boundaries.*

You are going to spend a large percent of your life at your job, so you want that place to reflect the love you have for yourself. You want to live and breathe in places that you thrive: your home, your work, or anywhere else that you spend a lot of time. It is your job to set boundaries within the spaces, and the relationships with people that are involved in those spaces, that align with your values. Speak up about an environment that isn't serving you or promoting your growth.

3. *Set relationship boundaries.*

It's okay to be frustrated, but it's not okay to stay frustrated. Frustrations within relationships evolve around recurring irritations—the dish left in the sink, or a certain tone of voice used. We find ourselves frustrated that this is happening over and over again, but we're not communicating about it. Your expectation for the person to read your mind in these situations is working against you, and you're ending up frustrated time and time again because of your lack of communication.

You are only treated how you allow yourself to be treated. When you set boundaries, you are teaching someone how they can treat you. If they don't respect your boundaries, it's not a relationship worth having. You will always be better off without a relationship that makes you continuously upset.

4. *Set self-boundaries.*

If you don't keep promises to yourself, don't expect other people to keep them to you either. If you consistently say you want something but don't do anything to get it, that is the example that you're teaching yourself. If you want things to be different and you want to live a life that you feel proud of, you have to stop disrespecting yourself by not honoring the things you say you're going to do. We communicate with ourselves all day in our heads. We have thoughts that race in and out of our minds and physical feelings of intuition. You have to honor what you know about yourself. The process of self-discovery allows you to set and hold boundaries in your relationship with yourself.

5. *Pursue relationships with people who are different from you.*

We put ourselves into relationships because of the simple desire to be connected and loved. We want to be heard, understood, and seen. When it comes to getting the things we want, we need to give those to others. Pursuing relationships with people who are unlike you allows you to build better communication skills. Don't discount someone because they are in a different group or come from a different background; you each have lessons for each other.

Chapter Summary:

- Your social health is dependent on what fulfills you.

- Choose your social circles based on your values.
- When you say yes to everyone else, you say no to yourself.
- Boundaries are required to have healthy relationships.
- You are in control of your calendar. Manage your time well.
- People only treat us how we allow them to treat us.
- Communication doesn't need to be controversial.
- Build confidence by showing up for something new.
- Focus on changing the things you can control instead of what's outside of that.
- Exploration allows you to build new relationships and show up for yourself.

CHAPTER NINE

INSTALL FOOTINGS - SPIRITUAL ANCHOR

Finding Your Purpose

Spirituality is very interesting to me. It's something that has countless definitions depending on who you ask. Spirituality, to me, is about connection. That means connection in all things—within ourselves and with each other as humans. I also believe that it's finding our purpose within our lives. I absolutely believe that every person has a purpose, no matter what you believe religiously. Every religion that I can think of supports connection and doing something that is bigger than ourselves. It's about being connected with a higher power and having a higher purpose to be a part of something that is bigger than us. This is why the spiritual anchor is about finding your purpose. This broad definition allows you to feel and be spiritual without checking a religion box.

Spirituality, for me, is working with purpose and having a purpose for every action in my life. When I connect with other humans and feel connected with myself, there is a ripple effect that connects to something bigger. Connection builds connection, and for me, it's always been about being connected to people and creating something bigger and more meaningful. I always want to become better because I know that I have the ability to create a ripple effect.

Some might not see the connection between spirituality and a career, but I do. I started working in a restaurant when I was sixteen years old. It's very easy—with late hours and being surrounded by food and alcohol—to participate in binge drinking without any judgment. In fact, you're usually judged more if you aren't participating. Take that from somebody who was completely sober for a year while bartending. I worked these jobs when I was sober because I took interest in the people watching, the conversations, and even the hustle. At no point during any of these jobs did I think that it was my purpose. I didn't feel a calling or any sort of excitement to show up. I was doing what most people do—just putting one foot in front of the other, trying to make money to survive. What I knew about work was that I had to do it for money. I was never taught to find something that actually fulfilled me.

In 2011, I made one of the biggest shifts I've ever made. I quit my bartending job and decided to pursue a fitness career. It was during a gym session where I was showing some exercises to a friend that I felt it. Like a knock upside the head. Woah—you can do this as a job. I had finally found two things I loved combined into the same job: talking to people and teaching them to do something that would positively impact their well-being. And so I pursued that career, and it was the first time that I experienced fulfillment. I went through the ups and downs of the fitness industry, but gained the opportunity to coach thousands of women struggling with their bodies or wanting to become stronger.

I started to shift away from the norm that was "fitness industry coaching" and to ask more environmental and emotional questions to my clients. It felt like a natural shift for me. It made sense to ask about stress and anxiety, as it pertained to fat loss. This led to discovering my true purpose.

In these conversations with clients, I felt this pull toward the connection that was forming. I started to feel less concerned with how people were moving and what they were eating and more concerned with just wanting to make their lives better. I started to dig in, ask hard questions, and refer people to therapy. This led me to where I am now, teaching women how to build a solid foundation that survives the peaks and valleys of life. If I hadn't taken the risk of quitting a job that was my norm and pursuing what actually felt good, I wouldn't be where I am. I believe that I'm living my purpose now.

It's scary to think about taking jumps when we're unsure. We have financial responsibilities to consider. But as I'm standing here (yes, I have a standing desk) writing this book today, I can tell you that I would do it all over again in a heartbeat if it would get me back here. I believe that many paths will appear in our lives, and that whatever we choose is the path we are meant for. Even when it feels like the wrong one. Sometimes we just need the clarity that comes from seeing the other paths out there. Our spiritual anchor can get us that clarity.

How you define spirituality is up to you, but for the purpose of this book, I'm speaking of spirituality as connection and meaning in your life. Connection is something that means different things to all of us. Some of us feel connected only when we are face to face, or physically touching, and some of us might feel connected even from halfway across the globe. It might be in the way somebody speaks to you that resonates or maybe just how you view a certain person in your life.

Above everything else, the most important connection is the one you have with yourself. The more you connect with yourself, the more you are able to connect with others—someone you know, or a higher power that you believe in. I don't believe that you can truly give yourself to a higher power without being your authentic self.

Finding interpersonal connection is something that people live for. Think of all the dating apps and TV shows centered around dating and marriage. We all want to feel connected. We want to be seen and heard. In order to find the people, or the power, that we connect with, we have to explore. Exploration, just like we talked about in the social anchor, involves building your confidence while building connection. It would be impossible to find our true purpose without taking a chance at some point. We first must connect with ourselves, and then we can truly connect with others. This means we have to let down our walls, even when it's scary. It means you have to walk on uneven paths. Those are the paths that get us where we are meant to be.

A lot of people have an underlying fear of facing themselves. We live in a world full of distractions. We are buried in our phones and constantly running from one task to another. People don't want to look at themselves because most people don't like themselves. If this is you, if you can't stand in the mirror and take ownership of who you are, you aren't alone. Distraction allows you to keep your walls up, and not have to come face-to-face with your true feelings or your true self. But staying distracted is pulling you from your purpose and from connecting with yourself.

You may not want to get to know who you really are because you fear the judgment that will come with accepting your whole self. But when you accept yourself, it brings authenticity that allows connection and clarity that leads to your purpose. Installing the footing of the spiritual anchor connects you with who you are so you can find what you are meant for.

A great way to start building an understanding of yourself is to learn what your values are. There are a number of exercises on this topic available online. Just search 'find my values.' This piece of self-discovery impacts everything else. If you don't know what you value at your core, how can you know what to base your decisions off of? More importantly, how can you connect with yourself?

Taking a look at the things you value is an eye-opening experience that builds connection and a greater understanding of yourself. It serves as a filter for choices, questions, and decisions. You know the things that are the most important to you, and you make decisions that reflect that.

In order to find your purpose, you need to know who you are. Learning about yourself and your values will allow you to be open to new experiences. You can explore your spirituality by doing things that align with your values. These paths can only be seen once you uncover yourself.

Many of us have spent a lifetime making choices that don't make us feel right. We tend to lock away those choices rather than look at them. When you start examining those choices, you're telling yourself it's okay you did those things, and that it's not who you are. Those experiences were simply lessons learned. Through this process, you can start to build that trust and belief in yourself again.

The spiritual connection builds as you understand yourself more and more, getting to see why and how you do what you do. All of this happens when you become willing to actually look at what is in front of you, and feel what you are feeling. You finally get to link the behaviors that you learned to the reasons you made those choices, and see how these still affect you today.

You will find your purpose when you are truly connected with yourself. You will also have more clarity and direction. Your purpose is your calling, something bigger than yourself—maybe even something you are scared to say out loud. Follow this calling. Even when the fog is thick and you can only see a few steps in front of you, you still have an idea of where you're going. You have an idea because you know who you are. You know your purpose. Let go of your shame to bring power to your present, and walk toward the light.

How to build your spiritual anchor:

1. *Get out of your comfort zone.*

No part of me wanted to ask for help again. I had worked with a therapist before and was never consistent. I took what I felt I needed at that time, and then moved forward (or what I thought was forward). When I sat down at yet another session, I felt like I was there to be there, but no part of me was actually present. The questions that were uncomfortable, and I didn't want to go through it again. But I did it anyway. I knew that I had found comfort in the discomfort, and my life was chaos. I knew in order to find a new life, I was going to have to look beyond what I was used to.

Getting out of your comfort zone might mean doing something new that makes you feel more connected with yourself, or doing something that's uncomfortable for you. It might mean you need to stop suppressing everything that you're holding on to. Whether it's asking for help, writing in a journal, or sharing with a friend—when it seems like work and it seems hard, do it anyway.

2. *Practice gratitude.*

I've lost count of the number of years that I've used a gratitude journal, and I can honestly say that it is the thing that has changed my perspective the most, within the least amount of time. Gratitude can be five minutes in a morning routine that can change the way that you see the world. It allows you to better connect with yourself and see the world through new eyes. A fantastic book to start with is called *Gratitude Works* by Robert Emmons. It explains more about why we need to practice gratitude. Beyond the perspective switch, practicing gratitude also helps you feel more connected. This small practice can create a shift in your whole life.

3. *Connect with yourself.*

There was a point in my life where being alone was my worst nightmare. I constantly had to distract myself with anything that would prevent me from actually being with myself. I'm thankful and happy to say that I enjoy being alone now. I am happy to be connected and know who I am, but it was a long road to get here. Connecting with yourself means taking the time to build a better understanding of who you are. This can mean finally signing up for therapy, life coaching, or committing to sharing yourself as you write in your journal. Your connection with yourself is the most important connection you will ever build. Don't ignore and isolate yourself.

4. *Respect your values.*

There's been a number of moments in my life where I've been what triggered. Something would happen and cause a spiral that I couldn't get over. This was a rough cycle of suppressing feelings and exploding later on that most of you have probably been through at one point. Once I learned what my values were and why I value those things, it was an eye-opening experience that allowed me to make connections with those triggers. By doing that, I could offer myself compassion instead of suppression. Learn what your values are, and then respect them. When we go against our core values, we disconnect from ourselves. Your purpose doesn't lie in someone else's values.

5. *Be introspective.*

I talked a lot in the beginning of this chapter about my commitment to consistent growth in my life. I will forever believe that we can accept ourselves *as* we are getting better, not only at the end result, because I believe that each of us can *always* be better. I know that I can always learn and grow. I will continue to strive for that, while also celebrating how far I've come. Being honest with yourself does not mean that you are hateful or unkind. It's quite the opposite, actually. When I talk about consistent growth and being introspective, it means being honest with yourself about your accomplishments, reflecting on how far you've come, and taking a look at where you are and where you want to be. It gives you an opportunity to create goals and figure out how you're going to get there. You can always be better, but in no way should you discredit how wonderful you are now.

Chapter Summary:

- The most important connection in our lives is the one with ourselves.
- Once we connect with ourselves, we can connect with others.
- Once we connect with ourselves, we get clarity on our purpose.
- Practice gratitude to understand being present.
- Connect with yourself by knowing your values.
- Learn to understand yourself by digging into who you are.
- Rebuild trust within yourself by walking paths you were scared of.
- Once you are connected, you are able to see why you do what you do, and where to go from there.
- When you become clear on who you are, you follow paths that are guided by that knowing, which lead to your purpose.

CHAPTER TEN

SEAL FOOTINGS

Creating Sustainable Habits

It's a pretty drastic difference, as you can imagine, when I look at my old life versus where I am now. Much of what has changed simply comes back to my habits—whether it's my daily habits, my weekly habits, or just habits that I have in general in order to keep me moving forward. Often, we just accept our habits for what they are, justifying things we do that we don't feel proud of as "bad" habits. At a certain point, you become defeated and convinced you cannot change them. You feel like you've tried everything in the book, but nothing works for you. I know exactly how that feels.

I don't think there's any coincidence that my habits were things that were self-destructive. My habit was to numb. This manifested in drinking, drug use, and distracting myself in whatever way possible. The original change in my habits was obviously sparked from my rock bottom. I knew that changes needed to happen, and I knew that I couldn't go on living the way that I was living. The changes that were required felt very big, but were actually made up of continuous small changes *also* known as habits.

The old daily habits I created led me to that rock bottom. The choice to continuously show up for alcohol, and not myself, was a habit. The lack of showing up for anything that would impact me positively is what kept me on my destructive path. There was a shift after I created a plan for myself in which I could finally sustain habits to keep me on the desired path.

Now, my mornings start with gratitude, movement, and coffee! I have a schedule that I follow daily to make sure that I'm working toward whatever my goals are at the time. I also commit to showing up as a mother, a wife, a daughter, and a productive member of society. In the moment where I realized that I had to make this change, I knew that it was going to be a big change. I didn't focus on the overwhelming feeling of the big change. I focused on taking one step, one day at a time. This was with help from AA and NA meetings, of course. And that's what I did; I kept showing up to each day. The small steps became daily habits, and I was able to build to be where I am now.

When it comes to your habits, I'm sure that you have many that you would like to create, and many that you would like to break. Not a single one of us is fully content with our habits. Our habits are what we blame things on, our easy excuses. It's something that I hear over and over again when I'm speaking to women. "I just have such bad habits." "I can't seem to break this habit." "I don't know how to make it a habit." There are two ways that we need to look at habits. The first is the physical action piece, the plan that you have for yourself to create this habit. The second piece is what's underlying that's stopping you from breaking or creating that habit. Taking a look at these two things allows you to create something that is sustainable, whether you're trying to stop or start something.

Our habits can lead us to a very frustrating point. We end up in a crippling spiral of defeat. We try something, are not successful, get mad at ourselves for not being successful, engage in negative self-talk, and eventually we bully ourselves enough to try again. And then we start the cycle all over again. If this sounds familiar to you, I want you to understand this cycle can be broken. It is within your control to walk away from this defeat.

This is why habit development, and feeling confident in how to develop habits, is so important. I know that it's frustrating when you want to do something and you're not doing it. I know it's easy to beat yourself up for not following through, but the frustration that you feel with your consistency is something that you can tackle if you have the right plan and enough belief in yourself. Sealing the footings in our foundation requires practices and repetition. The things we repeat the most are our habits. To be secure in what we learn, we have to implement and take action.

When it comes to physical action, it's very important that you schedule out your time. Just like we covered with seeing your value and prioritizing yourself, your calendar is yours to fill, and if it's full of things that aren't for you, you need to take responsibility for that. Taking the time to schedule out your weeks and plan for your goals is time well spent. You end up less frustrated and more productive. That also relieves stress and anxiety. You're able to be more productive with your time because you know where you're supposed to be and what you're supposed to be doing.

When you're creating a new habit, it's absolutely okay for you to start small. In fact, I recommend that you do. Instead of saying you are going to read for thirty minutes a day, when currently you are lucky to read once a week, start with five minutes a day. You don't have to fall into the all-or-nothing mindset. When you do, you overwhelm yourself. You won't be consistent, so you'll end up back in the same place you started. It's better for you to schedule a ten-minute walk every day to start consistently showing up, or to schedule an hour for the gym when you don't even have a gym membership yet. Start small, build momentum, and then move on from there. Any step forward is still a step that counts. This applies for any habit that you want to create. Start with the smallest version of that habit, be realistic, make it accessible, and plan for it.

In order to keep building momentum, it's much less overwhelming to focus on the easier task. If you have this big goal of changing careers and you need to update your resume, get references, and hire a coach to figure out exactly which jobs you want to apply for, just pick one of these things and start there. Focus on the thing that you don't have to rely on other people for so you don't find yourself using that as an excuse. This is the classic "when X happens, then I can do Y" excuse. If a step isn't accessible, make it accessible or find a new step. Take that step, and then build on that. When you see that you're consistently showing up, whether it's a week of that ten-minute walk every day, or two weeks of getting up five minutes earlier for gratitude, you'll see a shift in the way that you feel. That shift is when you become aware that you're finally keeping a promise to yourself. You're rebuilding trust with yourself and starting to understand that you are a person who does what you say you're going to do.

A great place to start is with morning and night routines. Here we find an overlap of creation of one habit while breaking another. An example of this would be if you were lying in your bed on your phone before going to sleep at night. One of the most well-known ways to create better sleep is removing screen time prior to bedtime. But when you remove that screen, what will it be replaced with?

I highly suggest to all my clients that they bookend their days with themselves. You start and end your day with something that is fulfilling to you. I practice gratitude and movement in the morning before my kids wake up. Before bed, I do my skincare routine and then some reading. These are habits that provide structure and stability to my life.

As for the underlying work, there's always a reason why you aren't being consistent or why you aren't showing up for yourself. Most times we just don't believe we're worth showing up for. If that's the case, go ahead and reread chapter two again and meet me back here.

You're valuable as you are. You deserve to have things in your life that make you feel good. Another reason you struggle with consistent habits is fear of what will happen and who you will become. It's scary for us to think about what our lives will look like if we actually prioritize ourselves, work toward our goals, and participate only in things that are fulfilling to us. We become comfortable in our discomfort. We may loathe our job or our body, but we know what it looks like. We still wake up having an idea of the discomfort that we will face throughout the day, starting with habits we aren't proud of. I woke up each day without a schedule, without a routine—I only knew that I would end up drinking at some point.

When you're trying to break a habit, you don't have to be the hero. I recommend not restricting any foods from your diet unless you have to for a medical reason. But if you are trying to set yourself up for weight-loss success, it's okay to remove chocolate from directly in front of you while you learn to balance your diet. It's okay to not set yourself up to fail.

How many of you know about a little something called self-sabotage? I can see you raising your hand. Stop being the hero. You aren't going to win an award for staring at the french fries and not eating them. You don't have to prove anything to anyone. I know you're resilient, and I know you're strong. But at a certain point, we all break. Set yourself up for success by changing your environment to meet your goals. It's okay to make things easier on yourself, and it will help you in the long run to be more consistent. You can only go so long facing everything head-on, with no emotion, and just trying to get through it.

While on the subject, I don't mean to bring you down, but . . . you're going to fail. We all fail, and we all learn from those failures. One of the best things you can do is expect failure. It sounds negative and counterproductive, but hear me out. When you lay out a plan and expect yourself to follow that plan 100 percent of the time, you are setting yourself up to fail. If you set yourself up for success with the expectation of getting back up again when you fall down, you'll be able to allow yourself more compassion, keeping you on track for the bigger picture. When you start something new, make the promise of showing up for it each day—and on the days you don't, be kind to yourself.

Part of planning can be allowing for flexibility within your structured life. There are times in which rigid structure will work against you, and if you are too rigid, you will block yourself from opportunities to connect and explore. Planning for flexibility will allow you to see and learn what other options you have, while working toward the same goal. Building in flexibility allows you to accommodate whatever the situation is.

If you promise yourself you will strength train every day for thirty minutes, but then you go on vacation and there's no gym, you will feel like you are a failure. If you promise yourself to move every day, allowing the flexibility of how you will move, you always have options no matter what the environment is. Your excuse to quit becomes obsolete. Planning for flexibility also overlaps the exploration phase we talked about in the social anchor. Exploring and trying new things is important, as are your habits and goals. It's possible for you to honor both.

The fears that hold us back from accomplishing goals or creating sustainable habits are usually connected with triggers from our past experiences. It is your job to be honest with yourself and to identify those triggers. The more you learn about yourself, the easier life becomes to navigate. Just like how understanding your values can work as a guideline for your decision-making, knowing your triggers can help you to build an understanding of where you need to be.

At the end of the day, your self-worth is always going to be very apparent in your habits. If you don't respect and honor yourself, if you don't believe in yourself, or if you aren't respecting your values, it's likely that you won't be consistent with your habits. When the mornings come where you don't want to get out of bed and move your body, this is where discipline shows up. This is where you are tied to your purpose and you have to remind yourself of the bigger picture. Underneath that discipline is your self-worth. You get out of bed every day knowing how good you feel every time you move, and knowing that you're worth that feeling. You repeat this until you believe it.

Anytime you are thinking of creating or breaking a habit, I want you to think of the two components: physical and mental. I want you to ask yourself what physical action steps you need and what plan you need to create, but also what the struggle will be with creating or stopping this habit. Is there fear that you weren't aware of? Is there a past experience that you need help looking deeper into with therapy?

Remember, the first component is the physical action steps, and the second is the underlying emotion that comes with creating or breaking that habit. If you don't consider both, the plan won't be successful. At some point, you will recognize that you need help. Help, support, and accountability can be the necessary first steps to creating or breaking your habits. You can find help exploring things from your past in therapy, or through hiring someone like me to help you plan out steps to take.

Recognize the effort that you're making, and praise yourself whenever you fall off, because you will fall off. It's important that you react with kindness instead of hate. Learn from the times where you fall down, and remember that you have fallen down before and gotten up again. You've made it through every bad day and every hard transition so far. You're still here. Whenever you reach the place where your habits are solid, you start to build momentum and recognize that you are reaching the goals that you're setting for yourself.

Motivation will lead to consistency, which will lead to discipline. On any given day, at least one of these will show up for you—as long as you believe that you are worth showing up for.

How to better your habits:

1. *To break a habit, remove it.*

I had to completely remove alcohol from my life for a year to see if I was capable of handling life sober. I still to this day believe that my success wouldn't have been the same, or even lasted, if I didn't remove that habit. This goes right along with what self-help expert James Clear talks about in *Atomic Habits;* if you want to stop doing something, then stop giving it to yourself. If you have a shopping addiction, delete the apps from your phone that you are shopping on. If you're trying to end a relationship, block the phone number. If you can't remove it, do whatever you need to do in order to create physical space between you and the thing, person, or habit that you're trying to break.

2. *To create a habit, make it easily available.*

We like actions that are easy. If you want to create a habit that will be sustainable for you, make it as easy as possible. Don't expect yourself to drive an hour to a gym if you want to work out but timing is an issue. Buy some equipment for your home, lay out your workout clothes the night before, and put them next to your toothbrush so you'll see them. Make things available and easily accessible. This will help when negative self-talk or excuses come up. I tried to talk myself out of hopping on my Peloton many times during a challenge I gave to myself of thirty-minute rides for thirty days straight. I would find myself developing a case as to why I wasn't going to ride that day, but I showed up, and I clipped in. I made the goal to clip in for thirty days because I knew once I was on the bike I would get it done.

3. *Set yourself up ahead of time.*

Create routines and schedules. I can't say this enough: You can't just wing it day to day. If you don't have a routine or schedule to follow, start with a simple to-do list. That's a small step, but you need to have some sort of visual and physical reminder of what you want to accomplish. Creating a plan ahead of time will allow you to know what steps are necessary and feel more confident in where to take action. If you want to practice gratitude every morning, and you drink coffee, put your gratitude journal next to the coffee maker. Every Friday, I lay out my schedule for the week ahead. It takes me less than half an hour, and it saves me by giving me a guideline to follow throughout the week so I'm not distracting myself with mindless tasks.

4. *Ask for accountability.*

Speak what you're trying to do out loud. You can tell a friend, a partner, or whoever might listen. Write down your plan and how you're going to do it, and then ask for the help you need. Accountability is the reason why so many people sign up for coaching, and are successful with coaches, but then fall off when the coaching is done. A good coach will give you the skills to keep following through when your time with them is over. Accountability is an important step that can get you started, but you have to build your confidence and self-worth to keep going. My clients call me the "pusher." I am the friend that climbs the mountain to jump into the lake with you and pushes you off first when you are scared. Once you see that you survived the jump, you know you can jump yourself.

5. ***Build your momentum by starting easy.***

Remember that you don't have to struggle through everything. You don't have to take the big jump right off the bat. It's okay to start with the thing that's right in front of you. You're going to be more consistent and more likely to take the step when it's right in front of you. When we look at all the steps together, we get overwhelmed. Start small with whatever you can and whatever is available. It's a small step, but it's a step in the right direction that you can feel good about. When you feel good, you get to build on that feeling, and that's the momentum that you want. Take the steps that the person you want to be would take.

Chapter Summary:

- Your frustration with consistency is linked to your expectations of what consistency is.
- Schedule your habits like appointments.
- Start with the step that's in front of you to build momentum.
- Create a morning and nightly routine.
- Plan for flexibility.
- Focus on the easy, doable task first.
- Work with both pieces of the puzzle: physical action and underlying work.
- Ask for help and accountability.
- Motivation, consistency, and discipline all work together.

CHAPTER ELEVEN

BUILD WALLS

Continuing Your Momentum

One of my biggest downfalls is the inability to slow down. I value my productivity very much, and I've had to really force myself in the last couple of years to take breaks. I have had to refocus and make sure that I am participating in my business practices that are most fulfilling. This has required me to ask for help by hiring a team of people. One of the most important things that I do now is reflect regularly on where I am and where I'm going. This allows me to make sure that I am taking action that aligns with where I say I want to go. It requires me to be honest with myself about where I am, and even congratulate myself when it feels uncomfortable to do so. I, too, have fallen into the all-or-nothing mindset, and it's easy for me to burn out. I'm realizing more and more the benefits of slowing down, even to the extent of having the words, "Stillness is productivity," on my desk.

For so long, I thought I had to prove my value through my productivity. I believed that in order to be taken seriously I had to work harder than anyone else. It's a common problem for women, and especially women who love their jobs.

I can easily spend my day talking to clients, developing new projects to guide them, and teaching about the hope that I want them to feel, but I always have to remind myself to lead by example. It's important for you to know that regardless of the experiences I've had and the lessons that I teach, I am *so* human. I strive for perfection, even while knowing "perfect" is a lie. When I was coming out of my darkness after hitting rock bottom, my momentum and reflection looked different than it does now. The process of slowing down to recognize where you are is a step that can't be skipped.

It doesn't matter what your steps are; it doesn't matter the pace of your momentum—all that matters is that you're moving in the direction that you want to. It's easy to get caught in the day-to-day, but bring yourself back to the bigger picture. Take a look at where you were a year ago, five years ago. Are you moving in a direction that feels good to you? Building walls around your solid foundation isn't to keep people out; it's to keep you protected and secure as you continue to grow.

By seeing where I am and being honest with myself, I can take any necessary steps to continue in the direction of my choice. When I was coming out of my darkness, sometimes the only step I could take was getting out of bed that day. It was enough at that time. I recognized that I was building momentum. I want to teach you how to reflect and build momentum as well.

Reflect

One of the most important parts of reflection is looking back on the things you've said you're going to do. If you aren't doing them, there's a reason why. Uncovering that reason can give you a solution as to how you can actually *do* what you *say* you're going to do. I have talked to thousands of women who struggle with the cycle of starting and stopping, and a common occurrence is that there's something unsustainable in the behavior pattern or expectation. If you catch yourself in this cycle, you need to check your expectations and think about what you need to do differently. This is where honesty plays the biggest role. Only you can recognize when you aren't moving in the direction you set out for.

By reflecting, you can sometimes see that your goals change, depending on what you really want in life. I wouldn't be surprised if, as you continue to gain clarity through this book, some of your previous goals aren't in line with your values anymore.

Goals change, but when a goal isn't being reached, it's usually the plan that needs changing, not the goal. That's if you created a plan or outlined the steps at all. You can ask yourself: Was the goal actually too big? Or did you just not make a plan? And if you made a plan, was the plan too difficult, or are you just fearful?

Maybe the answer is that you just need help in order to accomplish that goal. As we talked about, asking for help is one of the most powerful things you can do. I suggest that you reflect back at least monthly on the goals you set for yourself.

One way that I do monthly and yearly reflection is simply writing all my goals and the steps for that goal down in a journal. Seeing them allows you to take a very honest look at what you need to change, and what that change will require. If you have created habits that you started while reading this book and something feels off, maybe you've made it too difficult with the all-or-nothing mindset right out of the gate. See if you can change the plan instead of removing the goal. Laying out your calendar each week is a different kind of reflection. If you put something in your schedule that you didn't accomplish, why wasn't it accomplished? Does it need to be moved to a different time, or a longer time slot? Do you need to ask for help in order to accomplish that task? Creating the visual within a calendar is a reflection each week for you.

Use the habit chapter to create a more sustainable plan and set yourself up for success. Regularly checking in with your goals is a form of reflection that allows you to have consistent growth.

When you reflect, you think about how fulfilled you are. This forces you to look at yourself and where you are right now. You can create something simple—a weekly rating scale is a great way to reflect and check in. Are you drained or exhausted, and if so, how can you change that? Do you feel proud or disappointed? What did you do well? It's also an opportunity to question what you are spending your time doing and if you are honoring yourself. The goals you create need to include fulfillment—don't create your goals based on what someone else wants for you because you won't be consistent with them. If you think that someone will love or approve of you more if you change a certain behavior, your work will never be done.

Reflecting regularly allows you to connect with yourself and see how hard you are working, even when you feel like you aren't. We are very tough, and sometimes unkind to ourselves, so making a habit out of bringing the things we are doing well to the front of our minds forces us to see them.

Momentum

If you want to continue to build momentum in your life, you have to let go of the all-or-nothing mindset. I can't stress this enough. It is one of the biggest things that holds people back from having the life they want. Having the unrealistic expectation to be perfect and do every task at the maximum ability isn't realistic. Furthermore, it's just setting you up to fail. This is a self-sabotage cycle that many fall into. You might recognize it as telling yourself you are going to do something while already knowing you aren't going to do it.

Building momentum starts with one step, and you build on each step. If that means a five-minute walk in order to hit a 10K run goal, that's okay. It doesn't matter which steps you have to take to get to the goal, or the pace at which you are moving. What matters is that you're showing up.

Momentum builds from reflection and creates a deeper care for yourself, and when that develops, you have discipline that helps you to show up even when you don't feel like it. A year from now, even on your worst day, you will be better than you are today because you are constantly evolving.

This discipline is an important part of continuing momentum because there will be times when you feel like you're walking through quicksand. There will be times where it is impossible to see that you are even making progress. There will be times where you even go backward and fail horribly, wondering what the hell happened. If you reflect, you can learn, and you will be able to see the progress that you made. Forward sometimes means backward. Progress and momentum are never linear.

As you continue to reflect and discipline develops, the effort that is required in order to complete tasks or steps lessens. An alarm that seemed to wreck your morning becomes an expected part of your day. A task that requires a push from your partner beforehand becomes something that you just do, because it's who you are. Your commitment to growth and love for yourself becomes a part of who you are, and it's built into the habits you are creating.

Even though things feel very hard to change at first, and you might feel overwhelmed, remember that there might be a hundred steps to the goal, but you can just do one step today. Reflecting regularly allows you to focus on what you're doing well. We can be so critical in how we speak to ourselves, and our beliefs about ourselves become our reality. When you see all the things that you're doing well, and you feel proud, you are more likely to repeat those actions.

One of the best ways we build momentum is by starting small. By completing a small task, we feel encouraged and keep going. Breaking the goals that feel too big down into smaller milestones creates many opportunities to check steps off. A big goal with thirty steps becomes a goal with three milestones that require ten steps each. Don't block yourself from building by allowing continuous negative reflection time.

On the days where you take one step forward and two steps back, pull back to the bigger picture. Daily reflection is helpful for this. We live in the moment of how we failed that day, but if we pull it back to the week, month, or year, we see we have failed many times before and come out with new lessons on the other side. Your relationship with yourself will improve. You will see that, overall, you are constantly improving. It doesn't matter how big or small your progress is; with reflection, you will only see progress.

If you are reflecting and there's no progress, you need to re-evaluate the goal. Every one of those steps backward holds a lesson. I encourage you to look at the failures from the week, month, or year and ask yourself what lessons you learned. It is an empowering experience to think that you went through something hard, got to the other side, and got to bring something along with you. There was a purpose for that experience.

Before I go over ways to build momentum consistently and reflect regularly, I want to remind you again that progress is never linear. If you were to create a graph depicting the path toward any goal, it would never be a straight line from point A to point B. There will be times when you fall down, and maybe even quit temporarily, but if you reach point B from point A, it means you showed up again and realized you were worth it. Consistency does not look the same each day, and it looks different for everyone.

How to build momentum and complete your foundation:

1. *Revisit goals monthly.*

My reflection is daily, weekly, monthly, and yearly. I have a different process for each of them, and the time I take corresponds with the length of time I am reflecting upon. I recommend that you do the same. A simple reminder at the end of the week of what you did well and where you are making progress, along with your scheduling, is an effective way to start. If you need to change anything, you have the opportunity to do so. This can set you up for a successful week. The bigger reflection periods—monthly or yearly—allow you to really examine those lessons and see how you can apply them toward the future. You can check in on your goals and create new goals that are crafted from the clarity that comes from following your true path. Make sure you write your goals down and reflect on them at least monthly and yearly.

2. *Set your schedule to adapt.*

In order to build momentum and move consistently forward, I've had to adapt to many other people's schedules, including my husband's and my children's. There is usually a point in the beginning that it seems overwhelming to try to fit everything into my calendar and still do what I need to for me. I know that there will always be life's challenges, but I have resilience and the agility to adapt. In order to move forward, I need to have a plan, and that's where my schedule comes in. When you set up your schedule or set your goals, be specific—but also be realistic and allow flexibility for life.

3. *Create a daily checklist.*

This is simple and very pleasing for us because we get the instant gratification of checking something off a list. You likely have multiple goals that you're working on in different areas of your life. If there are new habits that you are implementing and trying to build consistency with, create a daily checklist for yourself that you run through at the end of your workday or before you go to bed. For me, this is a daily habits list including gratitude, movement, and fulfillment. These are things I need each day.

4. *Be aware of past triggers.*

When I talk about building momentum, it makes me think of the times where I wasn't consistent. I remember being knocked off what I thought was supposed to be my path—I know now that all the paths that I ended up on were meant for me, but at the moment, I hadn't planned for any flexibility. Planning for things that trigger us or ruin our consistency gives us realistic expectations.

I remember before we had children, when we used to travel, my husband and I would always visit awesome gyms to work out, as that's very important to us. After starting to travel with my son Cameron, we realized that we didn't want to drop him off in a commercial gym childcare with people we had never met. So we made the plan to just be active when we vacation. Since we expected what would happen, neither of us were triggered or let down about missing the gym for a few days. Look at what's realistic for you and what obstacles could get in the way of reaching a goal, then see if you can plan around it or create a new plan that will allow you to adapt to it.

5. *Make it worth showing up for.*

There are many things that we don't really want to do, but we know we have to. We have more energy for those things when they are fewer, and when we are fulfilled. If you want to keep building momentum, you have to make sure that what you're asking of yourself when it comes to your goals and habits is worth your time and effort. You need to feel proud and rewarded for showing up. Organize a way of rewarding or reflecting upon your fulfillment when you complete tasks or hit goals. After training, I like to feel my heart beating, reminding me that I am alive and well. I take a minute to feel proud of what I just accomplished.

Chapter Summary:

- Change the plan, not the goal.
- If you are starting and stopping, check your expectations.
- Redefine what consistency means to you.
- Make sure your habits and goals are sustainable long term.
- An all-or-nothing mindset is a setup for failure.
- Your goals need to be for you, not for anyone else.
- Focus on what you do well so you can repeat it.
- Revisit your goals regularly.
- Set milestones for longer goals.
- Know that failures are necessary lessons.
- Progress in anything is never linear.

CHAPTER TWELVE

HOLDING ON TO HOPE

A Letter To You

After realizing that I didn't have a good relationship with sex itself—or even the conversation of it—I set up an appointment with a phenomenal sex therapist. In one of our many amazing conversations, she asked me to write a letter to my younger self. It was one of the hardest homework assignments I've ever had. While writing this letter, I discovered forgiveness and built compassion toward past Kelsea. I was able to connect my heart and my experiences to build an understanding of myself I didn't have before.

Since writing this letter, I've realized the power of writing letters and find myself often asking clients to write letters to themselves or others. And I want to end this book with a letter to you.

My dearest reader,

Every ending is a new beginning, and I don't believe the ending of this book is any different. My biggest goals when writing this book were that you would find hope in the pages and feel valued and understood. I've found myself in the position, many times, of wondering what was next after I learned something new. I feel the excitement of new information, and then wonder what to do with it.

If you haven't completed any of the action steps from the previous chapters, start there. I purposely put them in each chapter so I was not only filling you with knowledge and (hopefully) inspiration, but also showing you how you can proceed forward in your own life.

It is a huge step to buy this book. It is an even bigger step to make it here, to the end. Take time to recognize that accomplishment, but don't let yourself become satisfied with only the bits and pieces that stuck with you.

Having new knowledge is powerful, but it is your duty to act on it in order to become your best self. This book can't do that work for you. I am providing the roadmap, but it's your job to drive.

Start with just one action step, if you need to, and build from there. Don't let change paralyze you.

Remember to start small and build consistent momentum! Return to the chapters before this that you found yourself rereading. Those are the ones that struck your heart. They hold the most power for you. Read them as many times as you need to, but never let the reading and the learning of new knowledge distract you from remembering you are strong enough to take action in your life.

Continue forward by applying the action steps I've given you, but also hold and expand on the confidence you've built by finally feeling understood. Remind yourself that your timeline is your own, and there is no perfect scenario, life, or dream that you need to compare your journey to. You are beautifully unique and deserving of this solid foundation.

As a reminder, when you feel lost or stuck, here are your steps for building a solid foundation:

1. Pick a site. Choose yourself. Choose yourself over and over again until you see the value that you bring, until you understand that you are the most important person in your own life.

2. Survey the lot. Own your story—every piece of it—even when you fear what others may think. You are the only person with the combination of your story and your skills. You have the potential to change someone else's life by sharing yours.

3. Start digging. Create a vision and set your goals. You have limitless potential and can achieve anything you've ever dreamed of with the right plan and belief in yourself.

4. Install footings. These are your five anchors that keep you in balance: physical, intellectual, emotional, social, and spiritual. Follow through with your actions to keep yourself anchored and strong.

5. Seal footings. Create new habits that align with your values and break habits that are holding you back. Habits are the things that show up most consistently to drive you in the direction you want to go, so make sure yours are aligned with your goals.

6. Build walls. Reflect regularly and build momentum by starting small, celebrating every victory, and pulling lessons from any challenges you face. This allows you to be honest about where you are and make changes if you need to.

When your world feels shaky and everything feels off, know that you have knowledge to guide you. Use the tools you have in your hands. You are capable, and I believe in you.

Wherever you are right now is where you were meant to be, and I am so thankful that you're reading these words right now. My heart is full of gratitude for the opportunity to share parts of my story with you in a way that I hope makes you feel seen. It took me many years of talking about this book to finally take the steps necessary, but the timeline doesn't matter, because here I am. I stepped out of fear and into this journey knowing that you needed to read this as badly as I needed to write it.

If you only take one single thing from this book, let it be this: You are more valuable than you know, and anything is possible if you follow that glimmer of hope.

Thank you for reading this. Thank you for being here. Thank you for choosing you.

If you read this book and found yourself wanting more, I would be happy to talk with you about the work we could do together.

Please visit www.kelseakoenreich.com.

ACKNOWLEDGMENTS

I am beyond grateful for the team of people that stand next to me, and have always stood next to me. The process of writing this book was an uncovering of my soul with the consistent reminder that my own vulnerability would allow me to connect with others.

I would not have made it through this writing process without my husband's belief in me. It inspires me to keep going. I am thankful for my dear friend Mindy, who has been a cheerleader and my most encouraging friend. To all of my connections on social media that said they would read my book before I even wrote it, I appreciate you. To all of my friends who have nudged me to keep writing when I was scared of failing, thank you.

Thank you, Mom and Dad, for always doing what you thought was right. Thank you for loving me through each of my struggles and allowing me to learn and build my own confidence. You both taught me that the only way out is, most definitely, through.

Most of all, I am grateful for each person that brought me lessons in this life, for each moment of pain that brought me here. This book is a symbol of overcoming my struggles and turning them into my passions. Thank you for allowing me to learn, to grow, and to prosper.

Every person that has crossed my path has mattered.

ABOUT THE AUTHOR

Kelsea is a lifestyle mentor with a multifaceted approach to her craft. Her focus lies in helping women to find their strength and empowering them with tools for both the physical and mental benefit. This approach ensures a mental, emotional, and physical transformation. Her true passion is teaching women how to live confidently and without fear by implementing simple and sustainable practices that work for anyone's life.

Born and raised in Texas, she has a fierce high-energy style that she brings to her teachings. When she speaks, she is engaging and creates a specific vision for her audience. She now lives in Florida with her husband Eric and two children, Cameron and Brooklyn. Her path to leadership began in the fitness industry in 2011 working on physical transformations. She started her own company in 2012, as she saw the need for something greater to be achieved in that field. After years of working with thousands of women all over the world, she became determined to make a difference in a unique way and knew she needed to create a different path. She now breaks down barriers and goes after what she wants while teaching women to do the same.

Her unique ability to connect with clients has created transformations all over the world. Bringing her one-on-one approach to a larger platform enables her audience and clients to feel heard and seen. Her eagerness and determination to continue to rise through every obstacle has motivated and inspired many. Her story is noteworthy not because of her achievements, but the challenges she's faced along the way. She promotes balanced living and being the leader of your own life.

Can You Help?

Thank You For Reading My Book!

I really appreciate all of your feedback, and I love hearing what you have to say.

I need your input to make the next version of this book and my future books better.

Please leave me an honest review on Amazon letting me know what you thought of the book.

Thanks so much!

Kelsea Koenreich

References

Brown, Brené. *Daring Greatly: How the Courage to Be Vulnerable Transforms the Way We Live, Love, Parent, and Lead.* United Kingdom: Penguin Random House, 2012.

Clear, James. *Atomic Habits: An Easy & Proven Way to Build Good Habits & Break Bad Ones.* United Kingdom: Penguin Random House, 2018.

Made in the USA
Columbia, SC
30 August 2020